Places I've Been, Things I've Seen

Opinions on Everything

Ken Shaw

Copyright

ISBN: 978-1-961028-82-1

Dedications:

This book of Thoughts and Opinions is firstly dedicated to my Wife Jane, along with my friends, Family members, and all the many Mentors I have been Blessed to cross paths with.

Acknowledgments:

My sincere thanks go to my wife Jane, also, Ray, John, Mark, and Christine for their help in giving me information, advice, and confidence to complete this project, and get myself out there..

About the Author:

One of many intentions in writing this book is to Thank the many persons I've known, and the Families I love. They have been a wonderous, and generous influence in shaping my life. Preparing me to take responsibility for my actions, respect traditions, embrace the leap of faith, and expect reconstruction in the building of character, self-respect, and self-esteem.

I welcome this fragile chance to display what I have learned. Even more so, the opportunity to be vulnerable with the results.

I'm hopeful readers recognize, relate to, or possibly share my opinions. Whether they may align with or be contrary to what is written. In the end perhaps, a discussion is created and embraced.

These collected thoughts, created and recorded to word, will forever be available as a reminder to me or anyone, what often appears overwhelming, may be an adventure in disguise.

Contents

<u>INTRODUCTION</u>

*"Water over the dam often trickles somewhere
to make a return trip"*

Ken Shaw

CHAPTER I
PLACES I'VE BEEN

EMBODEN AVENUE

THE LURE, THE MAGIC OF THE BACKYARD BROOK,

SOMETIMES JUMP THE BANK, NEAR THE BRIDGE THAT WE TOOK.

VISITING THE BEEHIVES, WHERE GRANDPA SPENT SPARE TIME.

MAYBE EVEN GETTING STUNG, FOR HONEY SO SUBLIME.

THEN THERE IS HIS GARDEN, THE OTHER PRIDE AND JOY,

SURROUNDED BY THE FENCING, LESS CHANCE TO DESTROY.

THE SMELL OF THE LILACS, THEIR SHADE FROM THICKENED WOOD,

PROVIDING US QUICK HIDING, WHENEVER CHANCE I COULD.

HANGING OUT ON THE FRONT PORCH, RUNNING AROUND AT NIGHT,

CHASE ELUSIVE LIGHTNING BUGS, FOR SISTER WITH DELIGHT.

UP THE STREET, IRISH NEIGHBORS, ALWAYS WORK ON CARS,

THE BOYS REPAIR A ROADSTER, WITH OLE MICK AND BLANCHE IN CHARGE.

ENTHRALLED, CONSUMED WITH BASKETBALL, OFF THEIR BACKDOOR STOOP,

THEY TAUGHT ME TO SHOOT UNDERHAND, I FINALLY MADE THE HOOP.

I LEARNED TO PLAY BASEBALL AND SLEIGH RIDE DOWN THE HILL,

GLORIOUS CHRISTMAS, TO THIS DAY, I CHERISH STILL.

PICTURES IN THE DRIVEWAY, OF HOWARD AND MY DAD,

OF WEDDINGS AND SNAZY CARS, THE BEST OF TIMES WERE HAD.

ONE WINTER WAS SO VERY COLD, OUR BIN RAN OUT OF FUEL,

WE BURNED BED SLATS, AND A CHAIR, BEFORE HEADING OFF TO SCHOOL.

THE HOUSE WENT FOR TAXES, BUT A LESSON HERE WAS LEARNED,

NOTHING IS FOREVER, NO MATTER HOW MUCH IS EARNED.

GRANVILLE

THE ONE-ROOM SCHOOLHOUSE

THE BUILDING, IT STOOD THERE, SO SMALL AND ALONE,

IN A FIELD THAT SURROUNDED IT, SOME GRASS, A FEW STONES.

UP THE STAIRS, AS YOU ENTERED, THE OUTHOUSE CAUGHT SIGHT,

THEN TO THE CLASSROOM, UP AHEAD ON THE RIGHT.

ALL THE DESKS WERE STRATEGIC, KINDERGARTEN THROUGH NINE,

IN THE CENTER WAS THE COAL STOVE, ALL THINGS KEPT ALIGNED.

SHE TAUGHT WITH PRECISION, MISS HAMBONE, SO RARE,

THE BEGINNERS, THE YOUNG TEENS, ARE RESPECTFUL, AND AWARE.

OUTSIDE WE HAD MARBLES, RING A LARIO, AND TAG,

INSIDE WERE OUR CONCERTS AND SALUTING THE FLAG.

MY FIRST CHRISTMAS PLAY, SNOW RAGED ON OUTSIDE,

THE SCHOOLHOUSE WAS PACKED FULL, WITH NO CHANCE TO HIDE.

MY MEMORY AND PRACTICE, CAME THROUGH WITHOUT FLAW,

THE FACES OF MY FAMILY, AND WHAT THEY JUST SAW.

MY LIFE AT THE SCHOOLHOUSE, WAS A GIFT TO BEHOLD,

FAR RICHER THAN MONEY, OR DIAMONDS, OR GOLD.

I DWELL ON IT OFTEN, AND WITHDRAW WHAT I'VE LEARNED,

LITTLE ONE ROOM SCHOOLHOUSE, STRONG CHARACTER WAS EARNED.

HANFORD STREET

ROCK AND ROLL HAD MOVED RIGHT IN, SKITTLE LEFT THE STAGE,

HAPPILY, I FOLLOWED, A KID OF A TENDER AGE.

AT TEN YEARS OLD, I FREELY ROAMED, A TRAIT THAT MARKS MY LIFE,

UNACCOUNTABLE FOR MY ABSENCE, WITH MY MOTHER, GRANDMA, AND WIFE.

ADVENTURES PEAKED THEIR CALLING, RESISTANCE ALL BUT LOST,

EXPOSED TO FRIENDS, GAMES, AND LESSONS, AT WILL, AT A HEALTHY COST.

TWO LITTLE LEGS, AND SOON TWO WHEELS, MORE HIGHWAY SOON IN SIGHT,

NEW MYSTERIES FOR EXPLORING, ABOUND BOTH DAY AND NIGHT.

HARDING STREET, THE CANDY STORE, THE SHORTCUT TO THE SCHOOL,

MY PAPER ROUTE ON WILCOX, A BRAND-NEW SET OF RULES.

BEVERLY DAIRY, LEMON ICE, A SHORT WALK THOSE SUMMER DAYS,

THESE SMALL JOYS MEANT SO MUCH TO ME, IN SO MANY WAYS.

FRIENDS ON WATKINS AVENUE, WE'D MEET UP EVERY DAY,

FOOTBALL, BASEBALL, COME ACROSS, AT Y.M.C.A.

LEATHERED POCKET POOL TABLES, PING PONG, SWIMMING POOL,

A YOUNG BOY DREAMS UNLIMITED, EVERY DAY AFTER SCHOOL.

MULBERRY STREET FIVE DAYS A WEEK, EIGHT O'CLOCK TIL THREE,

THE WONDERFUL MRS. DUBOIS, HELPED SECURE THE WAY FOR ME.

I LEARNED FRENCH, THE WALL STREET JOURNAL, THE WAY THE WORLD WOULD RUN,

THERE WAS NO "WOKE", JUST PROVEN TRUTHS, MY NEXT LIFE HAD BEGUN.

LEARNED SKATING UP AT DAVIDGE PARK, WITH MATHIS AND PAT BOONE,

SINGING ALONG, STRIDE FOR STRIDE, BENEATH A WINTER MOON.

THOSE MAGIC YEARS ON HANFORD STREET, FORMED MY LIFETIME CORE,

EXPOSED, INFUSED, THEN OPENED UP, A NEW WORLD TO EXPLORE.

HEY TROUT TOWN

HEY TROUT TOWN, HERE'S THE LOWDOWN

YOU TOOK A HEALTHY SPIN; YOU TOOK ONE ON THE CHIN.

HEY TROUT TOWN, HERE'S THE LOW DOWN,

TAKE AN ARTFUL CAST, DON'T REEL IT IN TOO FAST.

LET IT FLOAT IN THE SUNSHINE, FEATHERED LINE IN THE SNOW,

BRING YOUR NET THROUGH THE RAPIDS, IN THE CURRENT DOWN BELOW.

THROW YOUR ORANGE, OR THAT GREEN LINE, IN A JOYFUL ARC WITH WIND,

TO TARGET WHERE THEY'RE BITING, AGAIN, AND AGAIN, AND AGAIN.

TAKE AN ARTFUL CAST, DON'T PULL IT IN TOO FAST,

NET IT IN THE RIPPLES, MOTHER NATURE IS YOUR TASK.

GOODBYE ROSCOE, NOW THE SUNGLOW, TIME TO PUT AWAY MY GEAR,

MEET AND GREET THE LOCAL GENTRY, AND TELL THE STORIES WE LOVE TO HEAR.

HEY TROUT TOWN, THAT'S THE LOWDOWN, A SIMPLE LIFE OFF THE GRID,

WHERE WE'RE GUILTY OF WANDERING, WITH OUR TREK ON THE WATERSHED.

MELVILLE TRAILER PARK

THIS SAILORS SON WAS A WILD ONE, AT LEAST I THINK
THAT I WAS,

FOR I WAS ALWAYS NEARBY TO TROUBLE, THE REASON
ONLY BECAUSE.

MY DAD, MOM, AND THREE KIDS IN AN AIRSTREAM, TIGHT
QUARTERS FOR PARENTS AND CHILD,

THOSE NEW ENGLAND WINTERS, SPENT IN RHODE ISLAND,

WITH THE ARRIVAL OF SPRING, WE WENT WILD.

THE NAVAL BUS WOULD COME, TAKE US TO SCHOOL,

BRING US DAILY BOTH WAYS, THROUGH THE GATE.

ARRIVE AT MY STOP, TWO STEPS, OUT THE DOOR,

THERE'S MISCHIEF OUTSIDE, DON'T BE LATE.

BEFORE ME BASE HOUSING, TRAILERS ABOUND,

IN COLORS, ALL SIZES AND SHAPES,

FILLED WITH YOUNG BOYS, SO MUCH LIKE ME,

SEARCHING FOR ROADS THEY CAN TAKE.

PLAYING AND FIGHTING, THEIR FRIENDS ONCE AGAIN,

KNIGHTS SLAYING DRAGONS, AND MORE

THERE ARE CUB SCOUTS, AND BATTLES, WITH GARBAGE,
CAN LIDS,

DIVERSIFIED ATTRACTIONS GALORE.

NO NEED TO ACCOUNT FOR THE THINGS THAT I DID,

SO COMMON, WITHOUT NEED TO TRACE,

MY DAD WAS OUT TO SEA, MY MOM WAS NEVER HOME,

UNAWARE THAT I'D BE ANYPLACE.

WE DIDN'T STAY LONG, AGAIN WE'D MOVE ON,

OUR COMPASS FOR HOME WAS IN CHANGE,

ABNORMAL WAS NORMAL, MY LIFE AS A CHILD,

MY DESTINY HAD ALL BEEN ARRANGED.

NEWPORT (31 WEST STREET)

A WHITE PICKETT FENCE, SURROUNDED THE HOUSE,

WITH A LARGE WOODEN GATE, AND SQUEAKY HINGES IN AND OUT.

IRREGULAR CUT BLUESTONE, FORMED THE PATH ALL AROUND,

THROUGH SOME GARDENS, AND BUSHES, WITH SOME POSTS IN THE GROUND.

AMONG THE MANY SECRETS, OVER TIME I WOULD FIND,

WAS THE MAGIC OF HONEYSUCKLE, ABOUND ON THE VINE.

AROMATIC AND SWEET, A SMELL YOU COULD FEEL,

PLUCK THE PETALS, TASTE THEIR NECTAR, REMEMBERED PLEASURE SURREAL.

THE YARD KEPT MY ATTENTION, SOME OF THE TIME,

THROUGH THE GATE, DOWN THE SIDEWALK, MORE ADVENTURE TO FIND.

NOW ENROLLED IN SCHOOL, MY NEW HOME MOVE IS COMPLETE,

NOT FAR TO WALK, SEEN AT THE END OF THE STREET.

LARGER THAN LIFE, LIKE A PORTRAIT ON THE WALL,

LARGE BLOCKS OF GRANITE, AND WINDOWS SO TALL.

SCHOOLS OUT, DOWN THE STONE STEPS, THOUGHTS NOW OF PLAY,

RUN TO TOWN, THROUGH MANSION LAWNS, DOWN THE CLIFF WALK TO THE BAY.

THE SCHOOL YEAR HAD ENDED, AND SOON WE'D BE GONE,

ANOTHER PLACE LIVED IN; AGAIN, TIME TO MOVE ON,

HEADING ACROSS TOWN, ANOTHER HOUSE AND NEW PLAN,
MORE GREAT ADVENTURES, I'LL BEGIN THEM ONCE AGAIN.

NEWPORT

(JAMESTOWN BAY STREET)

THE FLAG IN THE PARK, UP AND DOWN ONCE A DAY,

WHERE PARENTS, AND CHILDREN, WOULD WALK THRU AND PLAY.

LOOKING OUT TO THE BAY, ENDLESS WAVES ARE IN SIGHT,

MY BEDROOM WINDOW CAPTURED A FULL VIEW, EVERY DAY AND ALL NIGHT.

A HOUSE WITH APARTMENTS, THE THIRD FLOOR WAS OURS,

SURROUNDINGS OF BUSHES, FENCING, AND TOWERS.

SIX STEPS TO THE SIDEWALK, THEN OUT TO THE STREET,

PASS THE PARK, TO THE PIER STEPS, THEN DOWN TO THE SEA.

THE BEACH, WAS ROCKY, A ROUGH PLACE TO STAND,

AFTER A SLOW WALK TO THE PIER, UP AHEAD THERE WAS SAND.

MY SISTER, BROTHER, AND I WOULD HAVE FUN,

WATCHING SHIPS FROM QUONSET POINT, DISAPPEAR WITH THE SUN.

OUR NEIGHBOR WAS A WAITRESS, AT THE DINER DOWN THE STREET,

I'D STOP BY TO SAY HELLO, SHE GAVE ME FREE FOOD TO EAT.

I WAS SENT TO THE BUTCHER, A CHORE FROM MY MOM,

WHILE USING THE SLICER, HE NEARLY CUT OFF HIS THUMB.

AT NOONTIME AT SCHOOL, WE WENT HOME FOR OUR LUNCH,

FRY AN EGG, JELLY SANDWICH, AND PEANUT BUTTER WITH A CRUNCH.

MEMORIES WITH MY BROTHER, RHODE ISLAND SUMMER DAYS,

TUBING AND SPLASHING AT THE PIER IN THE WAVES.

SOON TO LEAVE NEWPORT, AGAIN WITHOUT TRACE,

ALWAYS ROOM IN MY HEART, FOR THAT MAGICAL PLACE.

ONE HIGHLAND AVENUE

I KNEW THE HOUSE QUITE WELL, FROM MY HANFORD STREET DAYS,

HOW PROFOUND TO ME NOW, WHAT WOULD LATER PORTRAY.

ONE OF THOSE WINDFALLS, AS LIFE MOVED DOWN THE ROAD,

CREATING REINFORCED DIRECTION, TO HELP LIGHTEN MY LOAD.

I'D LIVED OUT ON MY OWN, GOING ON THREE MONTHS OR SO,

TEN BUCKS FOR JUST ONE ROOM, TO SLEEP, COME AND GO.

THE PAPER READ A KITCHEN, ONE BEDROOM, AND A BATH,

FOR JUST THE SAME TEN DOLLARS, AT FIRST, I HAD TO LAUGH.

THINKING MAYBE MISPRINTED, OF COURSE, I CALLED TO VIEW,

AFTER TALKING TO THE LANDLORD, INDEED THE PLACE WAS TRUE.

SOON I WAS PACKING, ACROSS TOWN NOW TO LIVE,

SURPRISED BY THE LOCATION, WHICH THE AD DID NOT GIVE.

SECOND FLOOR SO SPACIOUS, BEDROOM, KITCHEN, BATH,

THE TOP FLOOR WAS ALL MINE OR WHOMEVER ON MY BEHALF.

I'D WALK TO WORK EVERYDAY, A SHOESHINE ON MY MIND.

A QUARTER A WEEK, LOAFERS WAXED, THE EFFORT SPOKE REFINED.

CONEY ISLAND HOT DOGS, A LOCAL RESTAURANT OF MY CHOICE,

YOU RECOGNIZED THE AROMAS, THE GRILLMAN'S FOREIGN VOICE.

ALWAYS ON A BUDGET, REQUIRED SPECIALS EVERYDAY,

TWO DOLLARS BOUGHT OUTSTANDING FOOD, VARIETIES ALL ON DISPLAY.

YOU FIGURED IN A JACKSON, YOUR DINNERS FOR THE WEEK,

ONE GOOD MEAL A DAY WAS PAR, IT MADE THE DAY COMPLETE.

I WORKED AT SEARS AND ROEBUCK, THEN NORTH STREET LOCATION,

PLUMBING SUPPLIES, AND FENCING, FIRST ENCOUNTER FOR A VOCATION.

EVERYDAY THERE'S BREAK TIME, THAT COFFEE AT TOOTIE'S GRILL,

THE TOASTING OF THEIR CINNAMON BUNS, PERFECT TO ME STILL.

THAT YEAR IN '67, I LEFT FOR SAN ANTONIO,

JOINED UP WITH THE AIR FORCE, AND NOW REALLY ON MY OWN.

SOLD MY '57, MY 327 SHORT BLOCK PRIDE,

I COULD'T BRING IT, AND AFFORD TO STORE IT, STILL REMEMBER THAT SWEET RIDE.

I LEFT ONE HIGHLAND AVENUE, THE SAME AS I CAME IN,

STILL IN MY HEART, I STILL OCCUPY, ONE HIGHLAND WITH A GRIN.

SEPTEMBER AT GENUNG ST.

WHY IS SEPTEMBER THE MONTH THAT HANGS ON,

FEELINGS CONSUMING, MEMORIES GROW STRONG.

WEATHER RUNS SULTRY, OVERWHELMING WITH CLOUDS,

OUTSIDE IS CANCELLED, THE THUNDER IS SO LOUD.

THE WARMTH OF THE BEDSHEETS, THE COVERS, THE SMELL,

TOGETHER UNAVOIDABLE, THE HISTORY THEY TELL.

AT TIMES MOODS ARE DEPRESSING AND UNWARRANTED, SO
YOUNG

CAUSED BY COMPANIONSHIP, FEELINGS UNDONE.

REACTING TO PLEASURE, OFTEN CAPTURED AS LOVE,

FOUNDATIONS MISGUIDED, NOT FITTING THE GLOVE.

TUMBLING, THIS ROUGHNESS, UNEASY THE FLOW,

CONSUMING EMOTION, MISDIRECTED TO GROW.

SO YOUNG AS THIS CROSSROADS, ALREADY APPEARS,

RESULTS ARE DISGUISED, AND OUR FATE PERSEVERES.

ONCE MORE FOR ADVENTURE, FOR NEWNESS SO CLEAN,

ONCE AGAIN CLIMB A MOUNTAIN, AND SEEK THE VIEW OF
UNSEEN.

LONELINESS AND HURT, DIRECTIONS ARE BLURRED,

REBOUNDED FEELINGS, PREDICTION ABSURD.

A LOOK AT ITS ENDING, I LOOK FOR SOME PEACE,

EXCUSE HAS NO LIMITS, TO SEEKING MY RELIEF.

THESE TIMES IN MY LIFE, WHEN I MODIFY THE ENDS,

TO JUSTIFY MY ACTIONS, AND PART THEM AS FRIENDS,

THIS CHAPTER, MY LIFE, IN METAPHOR PRESERVED,

DEFINES HEARTFELT PATTERNS, TOWARD WHAT I DESERVE.

TAKE ME HOME

I'VE HAD MY BAD TIMES, I'VE HAD MY UPS AND DOWNS,

HAVE SEEN MY SHARE OF WORRIES, AND MY PECULAR FROWNS.

MY INSULATING QUALITIES HAVE SLOWLY DISAPPEARED,

THAT THICK SKIN, I CHERISH, ONCE AGAIN HAS PERSEVERED.

I CAST NO ILLUSIONS, NO TRICKS OF HATS AND SMOKE,

I TAKE THE CARDS THAT I AM DEALT AND TURN THEM INTO HOPE.

I'M LOOKING FOR THAT SPECIAL PLACE, WHERE I SUPPOSE,

THAT GARDEN OF EDEN SPACE, WHERE EVERYTHING THERE GROWS.

TAKE ME THERE, TAKE ME THERE, TAKE ME THERE, TAKE ME HOME.

THOSE OPTIONS OF REASONING, WHAT WAS WRONG OR RIGHT,

THEY TOSS AMONG MY MANY THOUGHTS, OF YOU AND KRYPTONITE.

I THINK MY PACT OF SOLITUDE, HAS RESURRECTED CHANGE,

MY SCHOOL OF THOUGHT, AGAIN RECOGNIZED, RESULTS CAN BE STRANGE.

TAKE ME HOME WHERE IT'S PEACEFUL, TAKE ME TO THE TRUTH,

TAKE ME HOME WHERE IT'S CAREFUL, TAKE ME THERE TO THE PROOF.

TAKE ME HOME TO MY REAL SELF, ALLOW ME TO FEEL,

LET EACH MOMENT I ENCOUNTER, GUARANTEE AS REAL.

TAKE ME THERE, TAKE ME THERE, TAKE ME THERE…. TAKE ME HOME.

THE BALLAD OF UNCLE BILLY

HE WAS A REAL MAN,

HE WAS A GOOD MAN,

HE WAS A MAN'S MAN,

THAT'S UNCLE BILLY.

HE WAS A COWBOY,

HE WORE A FOOTJOY,

HE WOULD MAKE ANY BOY,

WANT TO BE LIKE UNCLE BILLY.

WELL, COME ON JOSE, PUT YOUR STUFF AWAY,

WE WORKED HARD TODAY, YOU GUYS SURE EARNED YOUR PAY.

COME ON OVER HERE, AND LET'S HAVE A BEER,

NOW TELL ME REALLY, WHAT WENT WRONG TODAY?

HE WAS A FAIR MAN,

HE HAD A FLARE MAN,

HE'D TAKE ANY DARE MAN,

THAT'S UNCLE BILLY.

WELL, COME ON JOSE, PUT THAT TRUCK AWAY,

YOU GUYS WORKED HARD TODAY, I GUESS YOU EARNED YOUR PAY.

COME HUSTLE OVER HERE, AND WE CAN SHARE A BEER,

AND NOW TELL ME, BOYS, WHAT HAVE YOU LEARNED TODAY?

HE WAS A DANCE MAN,

HE WAS A MAN'S MAN,

I WAS A REALLY BIG FAN,

OF UNCLE BILLY.

HIS LEFT-HAND GOLF GAME,

THAT CLASSY BETTY DAME,

PUTS HIM IN MY HALL OF FAME,

GOD REST OUR UNCLE BILLY.

THE LIGHTHOUSE

STRUCTURED ON THE GROUND, FIRMLY ON THE SHORE,

STRONG AGAINST THE TIDES OF LIFE, REPELLING WINDS
THAT ROAR.

THE BEACON THROUGH ALL DARKNESS, THE HOPE AGAINST
DESPAIR,

A GUIDING LIGHT FOR ALL THAT'S LOST, CALM BUT
UNAWARE.

LASHING AT ITS SURFACE, UNRELENTING SUN AND WET,

IGNORING ALL IMPAILING FORCES, REFUSING TO RELENT.

SUNNY DAYS SO SCENIC, THE STORMY NIGHTS AND SCARES,

THE ALWAYS SHINING BEACON, THE SHORELINE NOT
IMPAIRED.

A PERFECT FORM OF BEAUTY, TO FUNCTION WITH ITS
SHORE,

SERVING AS THE LIFELINE, DISASTER CAN'T IGNORE.

SHINE ON AFTER SUNSET TO THOSE TRAVELERS WHO
EMBARK,

LIGHT TO ALL THAT WANDERS, WHO JOURNEY THROUGH
THE DARK

THE 2ND TRESTLE

THE CROSSING IS LONG GONE NOW, WITH TRAINS, RAILS, COAL, AND TIES,

LANDSCAPED NOW, THICK BRUSH, AND WEEDS, BENEATH THOSE RICH BLUE SKIES.

WANDERING THROUGH HIGH GRASSES, APPROACHING TRESTLE ONE,

ENCOUNTERING THE PINEKILL BOTTOM, ONCE WHITEWATER USED TO RUN.

WALKING NOW FROM BANK TO BANK, DRY ROCK BED IN BETWEEN,

CONTINUE DOWN THIS ABANDONED TRAIL, WHERE HISTORY SURROUNDS THE SCENE.

EMBEDDED COAL, CRUDE TREATED WOOD, CAST ALONG THIS TRAIL,

LEADING ON TO A CALM ADVENTURE, MORE HISTORY TO PREVAIL.

APPROACHING MAJESTIC WATER, VIEW THE OTHER SIDE,

CALM, WIDE, AND SMOOTHLY FLOWING, ALWAYS WITHOUT TIDE.

APPEARING ARE ABUTMENTS, ON THIS BANK AND ONE AFAR,

BUILT SUBMERGED TO HEIGHT OF GROUND, SUPPORTED RAIL AND CAR.

CUT FROM LOCAL BLUESTONE, STACKED FOR MEASURED STRENGTH,

ONCE HELD GIRDER, TRACK, AND WOOD, ALL CUT TO PERFECT LENGTH.

HISTORY SAYS THE TRAINS ARE GONE, THIS TRESTLE SERVED US WELL,

WITH FISHING, SWIMMING, AND MISCHIEF, WHERE OUR CHILDHOOD SECRETS DWELL.

NOW VISITING WHAT WAS STRUCTURE, A STRONG PRESENCE STILL EXISTS,

I VISION TRESTLES, BLUESTONE STEPS, AND LIFE CROSSINGS THAT I MISS.

WHITEHALL
(GRANDPA AND GRANDMA)

THE BACK ROAD TO GRANDMA'S, WAS WINDING AND LONG,

ANY THOUGHT ON ARRIVAL, THE ROAD PROVED YOU WRONG.

THE NOISE OF THE TIRES, ON THE DIRT AS THEY GRIND,

THE SIGHT OF THE ROOSTER TAIL, OF DUST LEFT BEHIND.

PASSING THE SCHOOLHOUSE, SOON TO ATTEND,

STARTING ALL OVER, AND MEETING NEW FRIENDS.

NEXT IS A PIG FARM, THEN THE HOUSE THAT I KNOW,

FINALLY ARRIVE THERE, AND INTO THE DRIVEWAY WE GO.

NOW, GRANDPA AND GRANDMA, OPEN THEIR ARMS,

THEIR HUGS AND THEIR KISSES, THEIR ABUNDANCE OF CHARM.

THERE ARE PLACES AT THE TABLE, FOOD ON THE STOVE,

THE PUMP IS ON THE COUNTER, WITH THE SINK CLOSE ABOVE.

THE WATER FOR THE HOUSE, ALL PUMPED HERE FROM THE WELL,

STORIES OF THE OUTHOUSE, TOO MANY TO TELL.

ALL WATER IS HEATED, ON THE STOVE FOR YOUR BATH,

SURREAL ARE THE MEMORIES, I'LL TRY NOT TO LAUGH.

MY GRANDPA HOOKS A CHICKEN, IT'S HEAD SOON COMES OFF,

 DUNKED INTO BOILING WATER, THE FEATHERS SOON GET SOFT.

NOW COMES THE PLUCKING, TIL THE SKIN BECOMES BARE,

THEN STUFFING AND SEASONING, TO THE OVEN WITH CARE.

SOME MORNINGS WITH GRANDMA, TO THE SWAMP WITH OUR PAILS,

TREK TO MEADOWS OF BERRIES, FILL THEM UP AND NEVER FAIL.

SHE PACKS US A LUNCH BECAUSE WE'RE THERE FOR THE DAY,

HEADING HOME WITH BLUEBERRYS, WE'D TASTE ON THE WAY.

ACROSS THE ROAD IS THE ORCHARD, THE BOUNTY NOW THICK,

WE'D GATHER SOME FOR LAUNCHING ON A PERFECT POINTED STICK.

SOMETIMES WE WOULD FISH AND SWIM IN THE STREAM,

WE'D ENTER BY A ROPESWING, AND LET GO WITH A SCREAM.

THE WINTERS WERE FRIGHTENING, WITH OUR SHARE OF DEEP SNOW,

ARM AND ARM THROUGH THE FIELD DRIFTS, OFF TO SCHOOL WE WOULD GO.

MY GRANDMA CLEANED HOUSES, IT WAS HER LIVING BACK THEN,

FOR LOCAL DOCTORS AND LAWYERS, AGAIN AND AGAIN.

DECADES WITH GRANDPA, THEY DROVE BACK AND FORTH,

A POEM OF THEIR LIFE, TO HONOR THEIR WORTH.

COOPERSTOWN FOURTH OF JULY

IT'S COOL AND SO DAMP, BUT THE SUN'S BREAKING THROUGH,

WE'RE STARTING A FIRE, OUR FIRST MUST TO DO.

THERE'S GROAN IN AWAKENING, SO COMMON IN YOUTH,

SOON SMELLS OF THE BACON ACCELERATES THEIR MOOD.

EVERYONE CONTRIBUTES MORE WOOD TO THE FLAMES,

WE HAVE TO MAKE CERTAIN THE HEAT IS SUSTAINED.

THERE'S MORE BREAKFAST TO COOK, AND COFFEE TO PERK,

INCREASING THE JOY FOR ALL OUR HARD WORK.

THE KIDS HAVE THEIR OWN WAYS OF PASSING THE TIME,

TEASING EACH OTHER, IN THE END WILL BE FINE.

ADULTS SLOWLY TALKING, PREPARING THE DAY,

CREATING IDEAS AND A SCHEDULE WITHOUT DELAY.

ORGANIZE THE TENTS, SLEEPING BAGS, AND COTS,

CLEAN UP FROM BREAKFAST, ALL UTENSILS AND POTS.

MOVE ON TO OUR SHOWERS, HAIR BRAIDING FOR SOME,

THE GIRLS SEEM TO SEEK THE HOUSE ALL ALONE.

THE MEN ARE STILL HANGING OUT TO SIT BY THE FIRE,

WHILE THE BOYS TALK SOME BASEBALL, MAYBE PLAY IN AWHILE.

EVENTUALLY WE ALL MEET, DECIDE PLANS FOR THE GROUP,

GATHER ACCESSORIES AND CHILDREN, TO BE TIMELY ENROUTE.

OUR DAYS INCLUDE SWIMMING, PERHAPS A BIKE TOUR,

OCCASIONALY WE'RE INSIDE, IF IT'S RAINING OUTDOORS.

THERE'S EXCITED CONVERSATION, LAUGHTER'S ALL YOU CAN HEAR,

THE STORM IS THE WHITE NOISE THAT CAN'T INTERFERE.

WE CAN ALL GO OUR OWN WAY FOR SHOPPING AND FUN,

THEN MEET AT THAT CHOSEN PLACE, WHEN EVERYBODY GETS DONE.

THE FINAL NIGHT THERE'S FIREWORKS, AT OTESAGA SO GRAND,

EXPLOSIVE ROCKETS TO THE HEAVENS, YOU STRETCH TO REACH WITH YOUR HANDS.

THE NEXT MORNING BRINGS PACKING WITH ENTHUSIASM SUBDUED,

GATHER ALL OUR BELONGINGS, ALL THE TRUNK WILL INCLUDE.

KEEP THE WATER AND THE SNACKS IN THE FRONT FOR THE RIDE,

SAY GOODBYE TO FLY CREEK, EXCITEMENT SOMEWHAT SUBSIDES.

THREE DAYS OF BEDLAM, FULL OF WONDEROUS SIGHTS, AND CHARM,

FOURTH OF JULY AT COOPERSTOWN, BREATHE TAKING FAMILY ALARM.

CHAPTER II
THINGS I'VE SEEN

A CAKE FROM PHYILLS'S BAKERY

MAKE US A CAKE TODAY,

PUT YOUR HEART WITH OURS ON DISPLAY,

LET IT BE SOMETHING, NO ONE ELSE HAS SEEN,

IT'S OUR PRIME WEDDING PIECE,

MAKE YOUR CREATION ELITE,

BUILT THE LAYERS, WITH SUBLIME IN BETWEEN.

MAKE IT ROUND, NEVER SQUARE,

PILED HIGH IN THE AIR,

GIVE THE INGREDIENTS, ALL THAT YOU'VE GOT,

THERE'S NOBODY ELSE,

WHO'LL DO THE JOB WELL,

WE KNOW WE'RE ASKING A LOT.

SO, MAKE US A CAKE TODAY,

YOUR SOUL WILL BE ON DISPLAY.

CREATE SOMETHING, THAT NO ONE ELSE HAS SEEN,

PLEASE BUILD IT HIGH IN THE AIR,

SO EVEN GOD WILL BE AWARE,

HOW MUCH THIS CAKE REALLY MEANS.

ANYWHERE COUNTRY FAIR

A COUNTRY FAIR, JUST DOWN THE ROAD, OCCUPIES THE FIELDS,

SLOWLY FILLING UP WITH LIGHTS, AND JOYS TO BE REVEALED.

FIRST IN SIGHT, THE FERRIS WHEEL, MAJESTIC AS IT SPINS,

THE TILT-A-WHIRL, AND THE OCTOPUS, ALL CAPTURE PATRON GRINS.

CHILDREN DOMINATE THE SCENE, AS WELL THAT IT SHOULD BE,

CHASING SHINY OBJECTS, ALL PRESENT VISUALLY.

WE KNOW THE SMELLS, THE POPCORN, SOME COTTON CANDY TOO,

NOSTALGIA CHARMS YOUR WALLET, FOR YOUR PALLET TO ACCRUE.

ALL THE FRIENDLY YEARLY VICES OF THE FOODS AND DRINKS SUBLIME,

THE SNOW CONES, FALAFFLE, AND CHIPS WITH CHEEZE WIZ, YOU NORMALLY WOULD NOT FIND.

THE VENDORS WITH THEIR DRYGOODS, T-SHIRTS, HATS, AND GLASSES,

JEWELRY, PICTURES, RAFFLES, AND TOYS, ARE PITCHED TO ALL WHO PASSES.

THE SPORTSMEN WITH THEIR TRUCKS OF WOOD, REALISTIC ANIMALS ALL AROUND,

THE CHAINSAW COMPETITION IS JUST NEARBY, THE WHOLE FAIR HEARS THE SOUND.

MACHINERY IN THE FIELDS OUT BACK, I HIGHLY WOULD SUGGEST,

THE TRACTOR PULL COMPETITION, IT'S TRADITION AT IT'S BEST.

OUR BOOTH FOR VETERANS AND GIRL SCOUTS, SO THEIR MESSAGES CAN BE HEARD,

THE LOCAL POLICE, AND FIREMEN TOO, SO OUR SAFETY IS ASSURED.

A FAMILY ADVENTURE, STILL PURE AND ENTRY FREE

WHERE NEIGHBORS GUARD ALL CHILDREN, FOR A NIGHT OF SERENITY.

THERE'S LIVE MUSIC IN THE BACKGROUND, TO COMPLETE THIS MAGIC NIGHT,

SOON TO FINISH WITH FIREWORKS, AND TO AWAIT NEXT YEARS DELIGHT.

A WINDING STREAM

A STREAM IS SOMEWHAT LIKE A CHILD, CHANGING EVERY DAY,

COUNTLESS ARE ITS OBSTACLES, OFTEN ON THE WAY.

MOVING LEFT, MOTION RIGHT, MANEUVERS UP AHEAD,

SEEKING STRAIGHT WITH ITS MIGHT, EXPLORING FUTURE GRID.

OVERCOMING EVERY OBSTACLE, NO MATTER WHAT THE SIZE,

AROUND OR THROUGH, AND OVER TOP, OBSCURE TO COMPROMISE.

UNDERESTIMATION MAY CLOUD A JUDGMENT THOUGHT,

WHICH LEADS TO LOSS, AT TIMES OF BATTLE, ITS FOE SO OFTEN WROUGHT.

AS THE BODY INCREASES STRENGTH, UNHARNESSED SOON WILL GROW,

WE SEARCH FOR A STRATEGY FOR RESISTANCE, TO HELP REGULATE THE FLOW.

EACH TECHNIQUE WE MAY OBTAIN, HAS SHORT-TERM RESOLUTION.

SOMEWHAT LIKE "PANDORA'S BOX", WE AMPLIFY CONFUSION.

 WE LET THINGS ROAM TO SOME DEGREE, FREE OF SOME RESTRICTIONS,

EVENTUALLY, ALL THEIR TRIBUTARIES, FLOW IN ONE DIRECTION.

CALL OF THE WATERFALL

I GOT A CALL FROM THE FALLS TODAY,

IT SAID I'M FULL AND ON DISPLAY.

YOU SHOULD ALREADY BE ON YOUR WAY,

AS I'M RUSHING TO KEEP UP MY SPRAY.

RECENT WATER AT THE TOP,

NOW AMPS UP MY FLOW,

TO POUND THE SURFACE OF THE ROCKS,

STRETCHED OUT SO FAR BELOW.

I FORCE THE LAND TO WANDER,

SO STUBBORN, AT ITS WORSE,

UNRELENTLESS IN MY MISSION,

I'M SOON TO CHANGE ITS COURSE.

THE MAJESTY OF MY FROTH,

FULL FOAM-FILLED MIST, AND AIR,

PRESENT SURREALISTIC WONDER,

WITH WHAT, WILL IT COMPARE?

TO AMPLIFY MORE BEAUTY,

ALREADY QUITE PRISTINE,

TO CERTIFY WITH NATURE,

THAT I AM STILL HER QUEEN.

CHIMES

OFTEN WHEN I HEAR THINGS CHIME,

IT TAKES ME BACK SOMEWHERE IN TIME.

REMINDS ME OF PEOPLE, PLACES I HAVE BEEN,

SOME ARE OFTEN DISTANT, A FEW AROUND THE BEND.

A SEASONED WIND BLOWS THRU THE TUBES, MELODIC
SOUNDS THAT FLY,

ENCOURAGING OUR HELLO'S, SOFTENING YOUR GOODBYE.

THOSE CHIMING NOTES, SO PURE IN TUNE,

THROUGHOUT AND EVERYWHERE,

CHANGE THE MOOD, AND VERY SOON,

CLEAR NATURAL SOUNDS WE'LL SHARE.

FISHING AT THE SPRINGS

THE PATH TO THE SPRINGS, THROUGH THE CALL OF THE GEESE,

MY FISHING GEAR, CLOSE AT HAND, PERCHANCE SOME CALM RELEASE.

ONWARD TOWARDS LOCATION, TO CAST MY ROD IN HAND,

FOR WATERLIFE LINGERING, JUST BELOW, NEAR THE SAND.

REPEATING THE PROCEDURES, WITH LINE THROWN OVERHEAD,

HOPING FOR SOME SUCCESS, AS THE BAIT IS GENTLY LAID.

SLOWLY RETRACT THE LINE, CREATING ITS RIPPLED TRAIL,

CURIOUS FIN-LIKE CREATURES, TO HOOK SHOULD I PREVAIL.

MANEUVERING THE WATERLINE, THE POSITIONING IS ALSO KEEN,

SIGHT OBSERVES A NEW PLACE, APPEARING ON THE SCENE.

WATER TURNING DEEPER, ACCESS LEVELS ARE DENIED,

OPPORTUNITIES PRESENTED, ARE WHAT MOTHER NATURE PROVIDES.

TO GO THROUGH THE MOTIONS, AND ALL OF THE CAUTIOUS PREP,

SUCCESS MAY BE ELUSIVE WHEN PERHAPS YOU MISS A STEP.

COMPROMISE AND WORK, WITH LUCK THEY WILL COMBINE,

REFINING THE PROCEDURES, IT'S YOUR MOMENT TO DECIDE.

PACKING UP YOUR TACKLE, YOUR BOUNTY, AND YOUR GEAR,

THE SUN IS GOING DOWN, AND THE MOON WILL SOON APPEAR.

WHETHER YOUR CACHE, IS FULL OR IF IT'S NOT,

YOU GAVE ALL IN, ON THIS DAY, EVERYTHING YOU HAVE GOT.

HOLIDAY WALKS

AS FRIENDS WE TAKE TO WALKING, SOMETIMES ONE OR
TWO,

OFTEN MORE THAN EIGHT OR TEN, HAVE GATHERED IN OUR
CREW.

THERE ARE DOGS TO CORRAL, AND WANDERING CHILDREN,
INCLUDED IN THE COUNT,

ON A HOLIDAY, IT'S NOT UNCOMMON, TO BE INACCURATE
ABOUT THE AMOUNT.

THOSE LOST DAYS TO MAKE UP, DISCUSS ALL THAT WE'VE
DONE,

A MIX OF TALK AND LAUGHTER, ALL THE JOURNEYS WE'VE
BEEN ON.

VARIATION IN OPINIONS, ON THE CHANGES WE HAVE
INCURRED,

PERCEPTIONS AND DESCRIPTIONS, ON OCCASION, CAN BE
BLURRED.

HOWEVER, WITH MIXED CONSENSUS, THE GROUP QUICK TO
DECIDE,

AWARE OF TRADITIONS CHANGING, IN A SHORT TIME WE
ABIDE.

WE LET THE DOGS GO RAMPANT, BARKING ON THEIR WAY,

THROUGH ACROBATIC MANEUVERS, TRAINED TALENT IS ON
DISPLAY.

TWO OF OUR OWN ANXIOUS DOGS, GENTLE AND SO SWEET,

EMBARKING TOWARD THE MAYHEM, IN THE DISTANCE
SOON THEY MEET.

CELEBRATING TOGETHER, AS THE CROWD AHEAD
SURROUNDS,

SO GRACEFUL AND SO INNOCENT, IN MY HEART WE'RE TRULY BOUND.

THESE TREKS WE INSIST ON TAKING, THE SHARING OF ITS GOOD,

WILL FUEL OUR CONVERSATIONS, TO REINFORCE WHAT'S UNDERSTOOD.

LIFE STRUCTURE NEEDS TRADITION, TO REFINE THE OLD WITH NEW,

MAINTAINING ROOM AND POSITION, FOR LIFE THAT PASSES THROUGH.

A WALK WITH FRIENDS, THAT SIMPLE GESTURE, TAKES THE OPPORTUNITY TO REVIVE,

SOON REAPS THE REWARD, UPLIFTS THE SPIRIT, AND SIMPLE INGREDIENTS TO SURVIVE.

HUNTERS BIG OCEAN CITY RIDE ALONG 2022
(BLINKIN' SHOES)

HE HAD A PINK FLOYD SHIRT, AND A REALLY SHARP RIDE,

LOOK AT THOSE BLINKIN SHOES.

HE TRAVELED STRAIGHT DOWN THE BOARDWALK, WITH A PUSH FROM BEHIND,

FLASHING THOSE BLINKIN' SHOES,

HE GOT MY ATTENTION WHEN HE LET OUT A YELL,

KICKIN' THOSE BLINKIN' SHOES,

THE SOURCE OF THE NOISE, WASN'T EASY TO TELL,

YOU HAD TO BLAME IT ON THOSE BLINKIN SHOES.

THEN THE EYES BEGAN TO CLOSE,

ALL THE ACTION WOULD SETTLE DOWN,

ANOTHER DAY AND NIGHT WAS SOON TO COME,

HE'D SOON BE BACK, THOSE BLINKIN' LIGHTS TO BE SHOWN.

RAMONES ON THE SHIRT, BUT THE SAME SLICK RIDE,

GET A LOAD OF THOSE BLINKIN' SHOES,

ZACK AT THE WHEEL, FOR THAT ROCK STAR RIDE,

TO FEATURE THOSE BLINKIN' SHOES

YEAH, YEAH, YEAH, YEAH, LOOK AT THEM BLINKIN' SHOES,

OH MY, OH MY, OH, OH MY, GET A LOOK AT THEM BLINKIN' SHOES

LOOK, LOOK, LOOK, LOOK, LOOK AT MY BLINKIN' SHOES.

RED, WHITE, YELLOW, BLINKIN' LIGHTS,

MAKE ME WANT A PAIR OF BLINKIN SHOES.

I'M TAKING THIS WALK AGAIN

I'M TAKING THIS WALK AGAIN NOW,

THIS WORN PATH OF FOREST FLOOR,

WITH ALL MY STEPS, THROUGH ALL PAST WALKS,

NONE THE SAME, AS THE WALK BEFORE.

THE BENDS AND DIPS, THE SMELLS, AND THE NOISE,

IT ALL CERTAINLY, WILL CHANGE EACH TIME,

RENEW MY SPIRIT, CLEAN MY SLATE,

RESTORE THE NEW STATE OF MIND.

THESE TREKS ARE SOMETIMES AIMLESS,

THERE'S VALUE EVERYWHERE

NEW CLOUDS CONFIGURE, SHORELINE ALTERED,

QUITE SUTTLE, BUT YOU'RE AWARE.

AND IF YOU ARE ON A TIMELINE, THESE CHANGES CAN BE FEW,

YOU'LL PROBABLY MISS THE WHOLE SCENE, AND FOCUS ON THE VIEW.

SPECIAL IS THE TIME, WHEN UNLIMITED AND FREE,

TO PURSUE IN ALL DIRECTIONS, EVERY NEW CHANGE THERE COULD BE.

IN ALL FAIRNESS TO YOUR OUTING, THE RULES MADE AS YOU GO,

EXPLORE, ENJOY, WHAT YOU MAY GRASP,

WHAT NATURE WILL BESTOW.

INDIAN ORCHARD ROAD

DOWN THE ROAD, ACROSS THE BRIDGE,

CURLING LEFT, UP AND OVER THE RIDGE,

THE WAY SWEEPS RIGHT, GOING LEFT ONCE AGAIN,

WALK STRAIGHT, AND THEN PARKING, NOW APPROACHING THE BEND.

UPHILL IT WILL CLIMB, SO SLIGHTLY TO STEEP,

YOU DON'T FEEL IT'S RISING; WITH THE SERENITY YOU KEEP.

SHOWING ITS GLORY NOW, THE WATER IS IN VIEW,

ENCOURAGING MUCH MORE WILDLIFE, MOTHER NATURE ASKEW.

INTEREST NOW GAINING, YOUR PACE NEEDS TO GROW,

YOU FINISH THE UPHILL, OBSERVING WHAT'S BELOW.

ALL STREAMS WANDER CROOKED, THEY SEEK END TO FIND,

ANOTHER LOCATION, WHERE THEY WILL COMBINE.

WITH SIMILAR RESOURCES, TOGETHER THEY FILL,

THAT GLACIER FORMED BODY, OUR OWN BASHAKILL.

INDIAN ORCHARD SNOWSTORM

THE LANDSCAPE IS COATED, THERE'S TRACKS ON THE ROAD,

FOOTPATHS LACKING FOOTPRINTS, ON NATURES WHITE LOAD.

BRANCHES NOW HAVE THICKENED, WITH THEIR LAYER ADDED WHITE,

BLOCKING CLEAR VISION, OF THE HORIZON IN SIGHT.

MANUVERING OBSTACLES, NOW BLENDED WITH SNOW,

AHEAD ARE TWO WHITE BOULDERS, TO SHOW YOU WHERE TO GO.

IN TEN YARDS THERE'S TWO MORE, POSITIONED, BOLD, AND STRONG,

THE PATH GLIDES BETWEEN THEM, AS YOU'RE MOVING RIGHT ALONG.

THE WIND FIGHTS ALL MOVEMENTS, YOU'VE NO PLACE TO HIDE,

THE STORM IS THE WHITE NOISE, EMBRACING YOU IN STRIDE.

YOUR BOOTS REPELLING WATER, WITH YOUR SKULL CAP AND YOUR COAT,

AS YOU TREK ON TO THE WETLAND, WITH ITS ICE NOW AFLOAT.

DARK AND SLOW MOVING, WITH MIXED STICKS AND GRASS,

SILENTLY FLOWING, WITH A SURFACE MUCH LIKE GLASS.

THE TRAIL MARKERS WE FOLLOW, ARE GREEN AND SOME BLUE,

A COURSE TOWARD BACK HOME, MARKED ACCURATE AND TRUE.

A WALK IN A STORM, PROPELS ADVENTURE TO BURN,

SO MUCH IS DISPLAYED, SO MUCH TO BE LEARNED.

WHEN OPTION INCLUDES US, TO HEAD OUT IN A STORM,

PREPARE YOURSELF FOR THE WONDER, IN NATURES GREAT CALM.

LISTEN TO THE QUIET OF THE WORLD

SEE THE MOONLIGHT ON THE SNOW,

HOW MANY TIMES HAVE I SEEN THIS,

RIGHT NOW, I JUST DON'T KNOW.

ALL THAT I CAN TELL YOU, IS MY FEELING HERE RIGHT NOW.

LISTEN TO THE QUIET OF THE WORLD

THE WATER RUSHES FROM THE TOP,

ENDLESS FROTH FLOWS, FRUITLESS TO STOP.

SILVER WITH SUNLIGHT, HIGHLIGHTS, AND MIST,

LISTEN TO THE QUIET OF THE WORLD

SEE THE CROSS FORMED SHADOW, BY MOONLIGHT GLOW,

ON THE WALL, UP AHEAD, JUST BELOW,

WHAT NEXT ON THIS VENTURE, WILL I ALLOW,

LISTEN TO THE QUIET OF THE WORLD

HEAR THE LIGHT WIND, UNHAMPERED IT BLOWS,

TELLING MY SENSES, TO VERY GENTLY LET GO,

SO MANY THINGS FLOWING, AROUND ME HERE NOW,

LISTEN TO THE QUIET OF THE WORLD

WHEN I DIE, WHAT AM I GONNA DO

LISTEN TO THE QUIET OF THE WORLD

LOOKING OUT AT THE ISLANDS

CLIMBING UP, I USE THE RAIL, SOME FIFTEEN STEPS I SEE,

A PANORAMIC LOOK, AT THIS PEACEFUL PLACE, ABOUNDING SERENITY.

THE SKY INTO THE TREE LINE, CONTRAST CALM AND REAL,

OVERLOOK TWO ISLANDS, WHOSE SECRETS NEED REVEAL.

OF WILDLIFE FLYING FREELY, FRANTIC IN THEIR QUEST,

SEARCH FOR FOOD, ESCAPE DANGER, TO PROVIDE FOR THEIR NEST.

UNAWARE KEPT DISTANT, OF WHAT CAN CAUSE THEM HARM,

A NATURAL SENSED PROTECTION, THEIR INHERITED ALARM.

REGAL IS THE WATERLINE, THAT MEANDERS WITH THE SHORE,

REFLECTING ON ALL THAT WILL BE DISPLAYED, MORE INTRIGUE TO EXPLORE.

UNDETECTED STALKING, OF ALL THE LUSH TERRAINS,

EAGLES SOAR HIGH ABOVE, THEIR SPECIES TO SUSTAIN.

STEP BY STEP, I LEAVE HERE, I'M SURE THERE'S SO MUCH MORE,

TO SEE AND SMELL, TO TOUCH OR FEEL, IS UNAVOIDABLE TO IQNORE.

THE PATH WANDERS TO THE ROAD, THEN PAST THE WATERFALL,

TREKKING OFF, I HEAD FOR HOME, REBORN FROM NATURES CALL.

MANY QUESTIONS ABOUT THE WOOD

SOMEWHERE ON THE WOOD ROAD, YOU FOLLOW FOR A WHILE,

MEANDER THROUGH THE TURNS, YOUR STEPS CONSUME THE MILE.

WITH PUDDLES AND THE SOFT MUD, LEFT THERE FROM THE RAIN,

CREATING SLOW MANEUVERS, A PACE YOU WILL SUSTAIN.

THE SIGNS OF YOUR SURROUNDINGS, YOU KEENLY ARE AWARE,

YOUR SENSES ARE ON GUARD, IT'S TIME NOW TO PREPARE.

THE SCENERY BECOMING THICK NOW, YOU SEARCH NOW FOR THE CLEAR,

SOME SIGHTS ARE NOW FAMILIAR AND THEY COMFORTABLY APPEAR.

EXPLORING ON THIS PATH NOW, MOVING THROUGH THE WOOD,

DEFINE NOW WHAT YOU DON'T KNOW, AND REFINE YOUR UNDERSTOOD.

SIFTING THROUGH THE DEADWOOD, UPTURN A FEW ROCKS,

CREATURES SOON SCATTER, AND INSECTS ARE IN SHOCK.

HIGH GRASSES AND THE LEAVES, IMPEDE YOU ON THE TRAIL,

MEASURED IN YOUR PACE, YOUR NEXT STOP WILL PREVAIL.

THE SOONER YOU DISCOVER, THE DEPTHS WITHIN THIS WORLD,

TO MANEUVER IN ITS MYSTERIES, THE CONCEPTS YOU UNFLURL.

UNDERSTANDING WHAT'S BEFORE YOU, ALONE IS SUCH A FEAT,

TIME AGAIN RESTRICTS YOU, AND YOUR ANSWERS ARE INCOMPLETE.

THE FOREST OFTEN CALLS YOU, KNOWING YOU WILL COME BACK,

EACH ROAD YOU WALK IS DIFFERENT, THE PATHS ALL GO OFF TRACK.

THE ANSWERS FROM MOTHER NATURE, ARE ALL FOUND THROUGH HER DOOR,

IF EVER ONE BY CHANCE SHOULD CLOSE, FEEL ASSURED THERE ARE MANY MORE.

MY SPRINGTIME DRIVE UP THE MOUNTAIN

NATURAL PATHS LEAD THROUGH THE WOODLANDS, THAT ONCE WERE FREE TO ROAM,

WHERE SHORTCUTS LED TO HUNTING AND FISHING, HIKING, AND BEING ALONE.

RESTRICTED NOW, OFF LIMITS, VIEWED AS PRIVATE SPACE,

BUT STILL HELD CLOSE WITH MEMORIES, NEW OWNERS CAN'T REPLACE.

WOODEN POSTS, SOME STILL REMAIN, OPPOSING OLD ROAD DANGER,

SOON TO REPLACE WITH METAL RAILS, BUT OLD FENCING STILL REMAINS THERE.

ENCROACHED WITH BRUSH AND SCRUB TREES, ASSORTED CREVICE GRASS,

THE BLUESTONE QUARRY LINGERS, LOOKING HAUNTED AS YOU PASS.

NOTICING THAT THE NEW HOMES OUTNUMBER ALL THE OLD,

LOOK UP THEIR BLACKTOP DRIVEWAYS, WHERE DWELLINGS SOON UNFOLD.

PREPARING THEIR NEW LANDSCAPES, TO COMPLIMENT THE PAST,

ACCOMMODATE WHAT ONCE WAS, ASSURES NEW LIFE TO LAST.

THROUGH THE TWISTED TURNS, THE HILLS COME INTO VIEW,

TREES COVERED WITH CLOUD-LIKE SOFTNESS, THEIR BUDS AGAIN RENEW.

OPEN SPACES NOW ARE HIDDEN, A COLOR CHANGE IS NEAR,

ALL THOSE FOREST CREATURE MOVEMENTS ARE ABOUT TO DISAPPEAR.

SOMEWHERE IN THE DISTANCE, A LONELY WHISTLE BLOWS,

ITS FINAL DESTINATION, THE TICKET ONLY KNOWS.

EXTRACTED THROUGH THE TUNNEL, WITH THROTTLED ROLLING SPEED,

WESTWARD HEADING SOMEWHERE, THE ENDLESS TRACKS WILL LEAD.

MY VACATION HOME

SHE WELCOMED ME WHEN I WOULD VISIT,

SHE WELCOMED ME TO STAY,

AND AS THE YEARS WERE PASSING,

REINFORCING MY MIND CACHE.

OF CONSEQUENTIAL MOMENTS,

THAT FORTIFIED ENROUTE,

A PATH OF MOSTLY DAYLIGHT,

DECISIONS WORTH SALUTE.

SHE WAS SUBVERSIVE WITH OPINION,

TO OFFER OPTION BEFORE SEEN,

UNFORCEFUL WITH HER JUDGEMENTS,

GIVING A CHANCE FOR ME TO DREAM.

SHE HAD A WAY OF TEACHING,

WHERE YOU NEVER FELT BELOW,

IN THE ABILITY OF YOUR LEARNING,

NOR THE LEVEL OF WHAT YOU'D KNOW.

I'D APPRECIATE ALL HER INPUT,

LET HER KNOW SHE WAS A FORCE,

FEELING UNBOUND IN MY DECISION,

WHEN I FINALLY CHOSE MY COURSE.

SOMETIMES BACKUP, THAT SAFE PLACE,

IN SOME MOMENTS OF DESPAIR,

UNTIL MY LIFE HAD SETTLED DOWN,

SHE WAS ALWAYS THERE.

SHE YEARNED TO BE WITH WALTER,

FROM THE MOMENT THAT HE LEFT,

NOW ALL IS SETTLED, TIME IS RIGHT,

HER CIRCUMSTANCE WILL REACH ACCEPT.

PICKING UP TRASH ON THE SOUTH ROAD

I'M WALKING AND TALKING, AND TALKING AND WALKING,

THERE WAS RACING AND PACING, AND PACING AND RACING.

I WAS BLINKING IN MY SYNC, AND SYNCING IN MY BLINKING,

THERE WERE HANDS ON THE CANS, AND CANS IN MY HAND.

THERE WAS HITHER GATHERING LITTER, AND THE LITTER GATHERED HITHER.

THERE WAS PAIN IN MY GAIN, AND GAIN FROM MY PAIN.

I WAS PATROLLING AND STROLLING WHILE STROLLING AND PATROLLING.

WITH A SCENE TO BE CLEAN, I CLEANED UP THE SCENE.

I HAD WIND AND CLOUDS, WATER AND THE SUN,

THAT WAS SUCH A GREAT RUSH, FOR THE DEED I HAD DONE.

PERFECT MOMENTS

THIS TRAIL OF LIFE I'M ON TODAY,

HAZED BLUE SKY, AND WATER SCENE,

THERE ARE ROCKS, DIRT, AND LEAVES,

WITH TREES, MESMERIZE THE SCHEME.

THE BROWN OAK LEAVES AND CLUSTERS,

REMIND MY MORTAL RUDDER,

THAT SOMETIMES REST MUST SHOW ITS FACE,

IN PURSUIT OF LIFE AND WONDER.

THESE THINGS THAT COME TOGETHER,

ALL AT ONCE IN TIME,

THEY HAVE A STRONG AGENDA,

FOR POETRY AND RHYME.

WITH NATURAL CURIOSITY,

WE SPECULATE THEIR FATE,

WE CAPTURE WORDS AND MOMENTS,

AND HOPE WE'RE NOT TOO LATE.

RAIN WALK

THE DARK SHINE BRIGHTLY GLITTERS, ON THE ROAD AHEAD,

FROM THE PELTING RAIN, THAT THE WIND HAS SPREAD.

THE MEADOWS ARE ENDLESS, WITH FALLEN TREES,

VICTIM TO MOTHER NATURES UNRELENTING BREEZE.

THE WEEDS STILL COVER, THE SLOPES BROWN AND GREEN,

DOING THEIR BEST TO MAINTAIN THE PRISTINE.

STRONG ARE THE SMELLS, THAT HAVE TAKEN OVER MY WALK,

COMMANDING WITH INFLUENCE, OVERWHELMING MY THOUGHT.

THE FLOOR OF THE FOREST, NESTLED SOFT WITH THE LEAVES,

ENDURING THE PATHS OF MYSTERIES TO ACHIEVE.

THEY CARRY ON TO THE WATER, BACK AND FORTH WITH THE WOOD,

ENCOURAGE THE WONDER, AS WELL THAT THEY SHOULD.

WHATEVER THE WEATHER, OR DIRECTION I TAKE,

THE POWER OF NATURE WILL MAKE NO MISTAKE.

PRESENTING HER CHALLENGE, HER BEAUTY, AND LORE,

EVERY JOURNEY PRESENTED, UNLIKE BEFORE.

REMNANTS OF A STORM

REMNANTS OF THIS STORM, BLOWING OFF THE LIMB,

SPRAYS SPARKLING SNOWFLAKES, THRU SUNLIGHT AND DIM.

COVERING THE ROAD, THAT IS ROUGHED FROM THE PLOW,

ALL PATTERNS AND MARKINGS, WERE GIFTED BY NEW SNOW.

THE STREAMS ARE ALL BANKED NOW, DRIFTS DEEP AND WHITE,

THEY'RE FILLED TO THE BRIM, WITH DARK WATER IN THE LIGHT.

THE CONTRAST OF WATER AND A SNOWBANK PRISTINE,

MOTHER NATURE IS SCREAMING, HER BEAUTY EXTREME.

THE SUN IN MY EYES NOW, THE WIND MELTING THE STORM,

PREVENTS MY CLEAR VISION, TO ADAPT AND CONFORM.

SO STRONG AT TIME BLINDING, AS THE ROAD MOVES AHEAD,

FROM THE SUN ON THE SNOW, THE GLARING SCENE HAS SPREAD.

LEAVES BUNCHED WITH ROAD ICE, SOME MELTING HAS BEGUN,

DEADWOOD AND BOULDERS, NOW GLISTEN IN THE SUN.

THE SIGN OF" NO TRESPASS", APPEARS ON THE SCENE,

A CENTURY FROM NOW, WHAT WILL IT MEAN?

ALL LAND NEEDS EXPLORING, FOR ITS SECRETS AND CODES,

AN ABUNDANCE OF MYSTERIES, ON NATURES BACKROADS.

SHE'S LIKE A STAR

SHE'S LIKE A STAR

I CAN'T TOUCH HER, BUT I SEE HER,

EVERY WAY, HOW I LONG TO TELL HER,

THERE ARE TIMES THAT GO BY,

THAT I WISH WOULD GO MUCH SLOWER,

I GUESS I NEED MORE TIME TO KNOW HER

SHE'S LIKE A STAR

A QUIET WHISPER RAY OF BEAUTY,

HER TENDER SMILE, AND HER EYES THAT SEE RIGHT
THROUGH ME,

I WISH I COULD CAPTURE,

THOSE TENDER MOMENTS THAT SHE GIVES ME,

I GUESS MY PATIENCE AIN'T WHAT IT USE TO BE.

THERE'S A PART OF HER, THAT'S A PART OF ME,

I FEEL THAT IN HER HEART, THERE'S A PLACE FOR ME.

WILL I BE A FOOL, WILL I LOSE AGAIN,

SOMETHING SAYS SHE'S DIFFERENT,

SHE'S MORE THAN JUST A FRIEND.

SHE'S LIKE A STAR

A WHISPER-QUIET RAY OF BEAUTY,

AND HER EYES, THEY LOOK RIGHT THROUGH ME,

WITHOUT A WORD, SHE TALKS RIGHT TO ME,

SHE'S LIKE A STAR

SUPPER WITH FRIENDS ON THE UPPER PINE KILL

WE LEFT THAT NIGHT TO MEET SOME FRIENDS, AND UP THE ROAD WE GO,

JUST A SHORT RIDE UP THE MOUNTAIN, SO I TOOK IT SLOW.

REACHED THE DRIVEWAY, UP WE WENT, AROUND THE DRIVE TO PARK,

TOOK OUR PARCELS OUT FROM THE TRUCK, AND A DOG PLAYED IN THE DARK.

WE WALKED THE DRIVEWAY TO THE HOUSE, CONTOUR TO THE FENCE,

APPROACHING THE GATE BEFORE HER, SHE KEPT US IN SUSPENSE.

MOVING ON, THROUGH THE GATE, SHE ESCORTED US RIGHT IN,

BARKED, ANNOUNCED WE HAD ARRIVED, SO SUPPER COULD BEGIN.

WE TALKED AND ATE, DISCUSSED, AND DEBATED, THE NEWS THAT PASSED US BY,

WE HAD REFRESHMENTS, AND DESSERT, THEN LINGERED ON GOODBYE.

GRABBED OUR BOOTS, COATS, AND HATS, WENT OUT THE PORCH BACKDOOR,

HEADED BACK DOWN THE PINEKILL ROAD, FROM WHENCE WE CAME BEFORE.

THE PINEKILL

VIEWING THE ENDLESS LEAVES UP AHEAD,

THE OLE' PINEKILL HAS CHANGED ITS BED.

GONE NOW IS THE WATER THAT CAUSED ITS FLOW,

REROUTED WAY UPSTREAM, WHERE FLOODWATERS HAVE TO GO.

WALK NOW TO GRILLO'S, THE BASKAKILL ROLLS HIGH,

BUBBLING FROTHY WHITECAPS, THEY SPARKLE RACING BY.

AT THE RIM OF THE ROCK BED, FROTH IS TURNING WHITE,

CHORES OF MOTHER NATURE, HARMLESS IN DELIGHT.

THE CONTENT OF THE WATER, ABUSES EVERY STONE,

UNRELENTLESSLY CARESSING, WITH A CALM WILL OF ITS OWN.

HIGH BANKS OF CRUMBLING EARTH MAINTAINED ON THE EDGE,

ROCKS AND LOOSENED GRAVEL, SOMEWHAT REDUCE THE DREDGE.

WHEN THE SEASON RAINS HAVE ENDED, THE WATER LOSES DEPTH,

EXPOSING ROCKS, AQUATIC WONDER, WHERE SECRETLY THEY ARE KEPT.

THERE ARE POOLS WITH FISH, YOU GRAB BY HAND, OR MAYBE USE THE NET,

TO CATCH A TROUT, GRASPED BY YOUR PALM, A BOY WILL NOT FORGET.

AS THE COLD SETS IN, THE KILL ACCEPTS THE ICE,

LAYERS GATHER SLOWLY, A CAUTIOUS NATURAL VICE.

ENCUMBERING THE WATER, TO STOP AND BLOCK ITS MOVES,

SOMETIMES CAUSING PROBLEMS, AS NEIGHBORS DISAPPROVE.

THOSE SOON APPROACHING WARM DAYS, CHANCE OF ICE TO BURST,

IT'S BROKEN UP INTO CHUNKS AND BRICKS, DOWNSTREAM IT DIVERTS.

DEPENDING ON HOW THE STREAM FLOWS, SOME DANGER LINGERS NEAR,

LOOKING OUT YOUR WINDOW, MOVING ICE, BRINGS A TINGE OF FEAR.

SOON LEVELS GET NEAR NORMAL, THERE'S CALM REPLACING NOISE,

THE AQUATIC CHANGES, ALTERED STATE, REJOICE PINE KILL REJOICE.

THE SPACE BETWEEN THE TREES

THE SNOW MELTS DOWN THE HIGH SIDE, OF THIS HALF-SUNNY BACKROAD IN CROOKED, TRICKLING LINES, THUS FORMING IRREGULAR PATTERNS, AND OMINOUS SHAPES, THAT LOOK LIKE ISLANDS AND CONTINENTS.

OVERLOOKED ON BOTH SIDES BY ELONGATED SHADOWS OF LEAF PILES, SHRUBBERY, AND MULTISHAPED TREES, UNSYNCOPATED IN DISTANCE FROM EACH OTHER. ALLOWING RECLUSE, AND PRIVACY, TO ANY CREATURES LOOKING TO MANEUVER FROM SIGHT TO THE PASSERBY.

I WALK WITH THE TURNS AND STEP AROUND THE SNOW ABOVE THE SAND-SOAKED EDGE OF THE ROAD. CALCULATING THE LENGTH OF MY JOURNEY IN THIS SEMI-WILDERNESS. I'M EXPLORING IN A FRAME OF THOUGHT, AS SOMEONE WHO IS SEEING ALL THIS FOR THE FIRST TIME, EVERYTIME THIS AFTERNOON EXPEDITION OCCURS.

UNCLE LOUIE
(1915-1994)

I WENT TO A FUNERAL ON SATURDAY,

ANOTHER OF MY FRIENDS, HAD BEEN TAKEN AWAY.

THERE WAS TIME TO THINK, OF WHAT HE MEANT TO ME,

BUT I COULDN'T SPEAK, OR TALK, SENSIBLY.

I HAD A CHANCE, TO MAKE THINGS RIGHT,

TO CLEAR THE AIR AND CLEAN MY SLATE.

I CHOSE TO KEEP THOSE THINGS TO MYSELF,

THE CHANCE WENT BY NOW, I'LL HAVE TO WAIT.

MY MOTHER, AND MY AUNTS, HAD COME SEEKING A VOICE,

TO TELL THEM, AND MAKE IT CLEAR,

THAT A MAN WAS MORE THAN A STEPPINGSTONE,

THERE WAS MORE TO LIFE, THAN BEING ALONE.

HE LOVED THE METS, AND A BOXSCORE OR TWO,

THE STATS MADE HIM SMILE; THEY WERE THE GLUE.

THAT MADE HIM SO HAPPY, THEY GAVE HIM LIFE,

IF THEY'D "BRING BACK THE DODGERS", THEN ALL WOULD BE RIGHT.

HE'S ON A HILL, THAT WELCOMES THE SUN,

IT SEEMED IT WAS OVER BEFORE IT HAD BEGUN,

A TIN VASE, SOME FLOWERS, THE RAIN, AND THE MUD,

BLANK FACES ON CEREMONY, NOT QUITE UNDERSTOOD.

ONE MORE CHAPTER, ONE MORE VERSE,

WHAT COMES AFTER, WHAT COMES FIRST.

ONE MORE MOMENT AND SOMETHING IS DONE,

TO SHORTEN THE CHAIN, MY LIFE IS ON.

WHO WANTS ICE CREAM

WELL, WE MOVED AGAIN, AND CAME TO TOWN,

THE STORIES, THE LEGENDS, AND SCANDALS ABOUND.

POPULATION ONLY HUNDREDS, NO BIG CITY LIFE,

ATTRACTED MANY ON THE WEEKENDS, TO ESCAPE FROM THE STRIFE.

NECESSITIES PROVIDED, THE GOODS TO GET BY,

WITH THE POST OFFICE, GAS STATION, TWO DELI'S FOR SUPPLY.

THREE BARS KEPT IT BUSY, FOR THE OLDER THAN ME,

REFRESHMENTS FOR THE GROWNUPS,

WHEN CONVENIENT, WOULD BREAK FREE.

AS FRIENDSHIPS WOULD THICKEN, A STRUCTURE WOULD APPEAR,

ALL THINGS WERE DONE TOGETHER, THE MAJORITY PERSERVERED.

TUESDAY NIGHTS AT THE AUCTION, WHERE ALMA MADE HER PIE,

WHERE BOXES OF CONTENTS, RUBE SOLD ON THE FLY.

THEN THERE WAS GRUNDY'S, A LOCAL LANDMARK WELL KNOWN,

ABANDON, QUITE STOIC, A HAUNTING PRESENCE STOOD ALONE.

ALL AMERICAN FAMILY BUSINESS, LEAVING FIXTURES AND GOODS.

OWNERS DISAPPEARING, SHADY REASONS WHY THEY WOULD.

SCHOOLS OUT, IT'S SUMMER, WHAT'S NOT TO LIKE,

ABANDON ICE CREAM AND CANDYBARS, A MISCHIEF MYSTERY IN SIGHT.

THROUGH A BROKEN WINDOW, FOR A QUICK LOOK INSIDE,

AMAZEMENT OF DISARRAY, SEE THE HAVOC THAT RESIDES.

YOUR MYSTERY'S BEEN SOLVED, IT'S TIME TO GET OUT.

A NEW TEEN ADVENTURE, WE'LL SOON TALK ABOUT.

THE SUNDRIES WERE LONG GONE, THIS CLEARLY WAS SHOWN,

IF YOU'RE LOOKING FOR SOME ICE CREAM, MOVE ALONG DOWN THE ROAD

FOLLOWING MY SHADOW

IN SYNC, STEP BY STEP, I WALK AHEAD ON MY WAY. MY SHAPE MANUFACTURES ITSELF, WITH THE HELP OF THE SUN AT MY BACK.

IT MAKES ME TAKE THOUGHT.   HOW IT HAS ALWAYS BEEN FOLLOWING DIRECTION FROM THE GUIDE OF THE SUN. UNKNOWLINGLY PROVIDING A CONDUIT FOR HEALTHY CONTIMPLATION AND LEARNING. HOW THE SHADOW IS ALWAYS AHEAD BY A STEP, TO KEEP ME ON TRACK.

AS I RETURN, THE SUN IN MY EYES, AND THE SHAPE OF MY SHADOW DISAPPEARS. ONLY TO RETURN, IF I CHANGE DIRECTION, TO A PLACE I HAVE BEEN BEFORE.

SOME PROGRESS ON MY OWN, WITH THIS SMALL REVEAL AND DIRECTION, TENDS TO ENCOURAGE AND ASSURE ME, WHAT I'VE LEARNED FROM TAKING THE SUN AS A MENTOR AND INSTITUTION.   AN ETERNAL RESOURCE THAT WILL CREATE PERPETUAL OCCASIONS, AND HUNGER TO EXPLORE.

TREASURE HUNT ON THE BASHAKILL

THIS WALK IS MOVING QUICKLY, THE PLANTS TAKE THE STAGE,

EVERYTHING'S CHANGING, MOTHER NATURE'S NEW PAGE.

THE PATH NOW HAS BORDERS, DISTINCT IN RICH GREEN,

BIRDCALLS EMBELLISH, THIS WORLD OF PRISTINE.

THE CALLINGS THEY VARY, FROM CATCALLS TO SQUAWKS,

I'M HOPEFUL FOR ENCOUNTER WITH THE EAGLE OR A HAWK.

FISHERMAN ARE OUT THERE IN THE CATTAILS AND WEEDS,

IT PRESENTS SLOW MANUEVER, WITH PERSISTENCE, THEY PROCEED.

THE TREES NOW DEVELOPED, WITH A CANOPY OF SHADE,

HELP REVITALIZE MY ENDURANCE, AS CONTINUED PROGRESS IS MADE.

THERE'S POPLAR AND OAK TREES, NEW GROWTH ON THE FLOOR,

A REPLENISHED ABUNDANCE, IMPOSSIBLE TO IGNORE.

ELEMENTS STILL BREAKING DOWN, REMNANT RAILROAD TIES AND COAL,

PRESERVING THIS JOURNEY, NEVER TO GROW OLD.

TODAY THE FALLS HAS A DRY BED, STILL MAJESTIC IN ITS WAY,

PROJECTING SOME INTIMIDATION WITH ONLY HER ROCKS ON DISPLAY.

I RECALL THOSE MANY PAST TREKS WITH MY DOGS AND SOME FRIENDS,

SITTING DOWN IN POOLS AND RAPIDS, COOLING DOWN AT DAYS END.

THE SUN TELLS ME IT'S TIME TO GO, IT'S TIME TO HEAD BACK HOME,

EXPERIENCES I'VE ENCOUNTERED, WON'T SOON LEAVE ME ALONE.

MOTHER NATURE MAINTAINS HER BOUNTY, NO OTHER FORCE CAN HOLD,

IT TAKES YOUR TIME, THE REST IS FREE, ABUNDANT PLEASURE TO BEHOLD.

CHAPTER III
OPINIONS ON EVERYTHING

OUR WALK IS A WALTZ WITH YOU

THIS DAY IS OPEN WITH THE SUN, CLOUDS, AND BLUE,

STEP BY STEP ON THIS BACKROAD, I'M STRIDE FOR STRIDE WITH YOU.

OUR PACE SETS A METER, ENCHANTING THROUGH EACH STEP,

WE CONCENTRATE ON GETTING THERE, FORGETTING WHY WE LEFT.

IT'S OUR TIME TO RECONNECT, APPRECIATE AND SEE,

TO UNCOMPLICATE THOSE MENTAL KNOTS, TO SOME DEGREE.

CLEAR UP SOME QUESTIONS, SEEKING CLOSURE AND TRUST,

WITHOUT OTHERS TAKING INTEREST, IN WHAT WE DISCUSS.

MOTHER NATURE, HER SOUNDS, KEEPING UP WITH OUR WALK,

SEEMS MORE LIKE WE'RE GLIDING, ON THIS JOURNEY WHILE WE TALK.

IT'S ALMOST LIKE DANCING, IN HOW THEY COINSIDE,

TO RESIST SUCH A FEELING, RIVALS HOLDING BACK THE TIDE.

TOGETHER THESE WANDERINGS, OUR HIKES AND GETAWAYS,

WORKING SOME COMMON THEME, REPEATING DAY AFTER DAY,

OUR ADVENTURE IS OVER, NOTHING LEFT TO PURSUE,

OUR WALK ON THE BACKROAD IS ANOTHER WALTZ WITH YOU.

IS THIS A DEBATE

I'VE BEEN SO MANY PLACES, IT SOMETIMES SCARES ME SO,

CONFUSING VIEWS AND THEIR LOCATIONS, I DON'T KNOW WHERE TO GO.

ON THIS DAY, I AM PURSUADED, I THINK YOU COULD BE WRONG,

AND THOUGH WE JUST DEBATED, MY POINT OF VIEW IS STRONG.

THE TIME WILL PASS AGAIN NOW, WE'LL GET TOGETHER FOR AWHILE,

WORK OUT SOME SOLUTIONS, WITH OUR PAST DENIALS.

THE ROADS AGAIN ARE MANY, THE WORLD EXPLODING FRIGHT,

MISDIRECTIONS AND EXPECTATIONS, IMPOSSIBLE TO MAKE RIGHT.

BUILDING REVERSE PYRAMIDS, TOO OFTEN IS THE CASE,

SPECULATORS CHANGING PRINCIPLES, HOPING HISTORY WILL ERASE.

CALCULATING WITH THEIR INNER CIRCLES, ALWAYS PROPOSING SOME NEW PLAN,

OPPOSING ALL RESISTANCE WITH DARK RESOURCE IF THEY CAN.

SLIPPING THROUGH THOSE BACKDOORS, ONLY OPEN TO CHOSEN FEW,

THEY LEND SUPPORT FOREVER, SEEKING CAUSES WITHOUT A CLUE.

THEIR MISSION EMBRACE DISRUPPTION, UNLIMITED FUNDING AT THEIR FEET,

HOPING FOR INFLAMATION WITH THEIR POWER OF DISCREET.

WHEN THE CRACK HAS OPENED, THEY SEEK ACCEPTANCE AS THE NORM,

UNTIL FINALLY THEY SUCCEED, REEKING HAVOC, ENCOURAGE HARM.

SOON RECOGNIZED, THEY DOWNSIZE, THEIR FUEL SHOUTS ONLY SMOKE,

WHAT REMAINS IS THE WASTED FOCUS ON THEIR EMPHASIS OF WOKE.

UNRULY

UNRULY HAS SUCH LICENSE, LIKE A DAM IN OVERFLOW,

LIKE CROWDS IN THEIR UPHEAVAL, PASSIONS ON THE GO.

NOT RELENTING IN THE DISCOURSE, UNWAVERING TO NONE,

ITS SURFACE, NOT QUITE RECOGNIZED, A CHANGE HAS JUST BEGUN.

ALL THE SIGNS COLLECTED, LIKE SO MANY TIMES BEFORE,

WE DO A QUICK FIX, MOVE ALONG, THE SOLUTION AGAIN IGNORED.

THE TRIGGER ON THE MAGIC BULLET, IS PULLED TO MAKE THINGS RIGHT,

HOW OFTEN HAVE WE FIRED, WITHOUT LOOKING THRU THE SIGHT.

ONE HAS TO WONDER, AS TIME MOVES ON, THRU THICKENED BURIED PAST,

WHAT CAN BE DONE, TO STOP THE RAGE, WHAT COMPROMISE WILL LAST.

CHILDREN MISDIRECTED DOWN A PATH, WE HAVE TO QUESTION MORE,

THE POOR RESULTS, THE UNHEALTHY SCENES, FURTHER TO EXPLORE.

REPRESENTING LIFE, A PENDULUM, SWINGS FAR RIGHT, MIDDLE, LEFT,

A PRAYER COULD SWING IT TO THE PLACE, WHERE WE CAN ALL ACCEPT.

UNFRIENDS

AS USUAL, THE MOOD SWING, MOVES FAST AND SLOW,

DECISIONS TO FOLLOW WILL SWING TO AND FRO.

A PONDERING SADDNESS, THEN RESURRECTED HIGHS,

WILL FILTER THE MOMENTS, AS TIME PASSES BY.

ALREADY I KNOW, WHAT THE SOLUTION WILL BE,

TO THE PROBLEM BEFORE ME, ON THE TABLE TO SEE.

MAINTAINING THE HIGH ROAD, TO ANSWER THE WRONG,

EXCEEDS TOO MUCH HEAD ROOM, GOES ON FOR TOO LONG.

A PROCESS THAT REPEATS, WITH OBVIOUS ROUTINES,

DWINDLES MY RESOURCES, EXHAUSTING MY MEANS.

THE FINE LINE OF FRIENDSHIPS, WHAT OFTEN OCCURS,

THINGS DONE TOGETHER HAVE RESULTS ON A CURVE.

OUR BOUNDARIES CAN GET CLOUDY, WITH STRUGGLE TO CORRECT,

NEED TO GET BACK ON POINT, TO SAVE SOME SELF RESPECT.

SOLUTIONS TO SOME THINGS, QUITE OFTEN WON'T COME,

THE ODDS STACKED TOO HIGH, WITH THE PERSONS YOUR AMONG.

A FRIENDSHIP DOESEN'T END, JUST MAIN CAUSES TO SALUTE,

ELIMINATE THE REASONING, TO MAKE THEM ABSOULTE.

BY NEVER RELENTING, TO A KNOWN TOXIC PLAN,

CAUSTIC IN RESULTS, I NOW FINALLY UNDERSTAND.

TWO WAYS

TWO WAYS OF DOING THINGS,

YOUR WAY AND MINE,

WHICH WAS THE BEST WAY,

RESULTS ARE DOWN THE LINE.

TWO WAYS TO DO THINGS,

HIS WAY OR HERS,

RESULTS OF THE RIGHT WAY,

HOPE WE FIND OUT SOON FOR SURE.

TWO WAYS WE CAN DO THINGS,

WHO'S RIGHT, AND WHO IS WRONG,

THERE'S THEIR WAY, AND OUR WAY,

WHICH WAY WILL PROVE STRONG.

YOUR TURN, OR THEIR TURN,

IT'S MY TURN THAT COMES NEXT,

ETERNAL DISORDER ON ORDER,

GENERATION AGAIN PERPLEXED.

WAKIN' UP

BOTTLED WATER ON THE TABLE, MY GLASSES LAY CLOSE BY,

MY PISTOL ON THE SHELF BELOW, MY BODY'S ON THE RISE.

SOMETIMES IN THE DARKNESS, MOSTLY IN THE LIGHT,

MY EYES SO FAR HAVE OPENED, TO MY CALM DELIGHT.

LIKE MOST I START WITH COFFEE, IT'S SOMEWHERE TO BEGIN,

I'M NOT QUITE YET, UP TO SPEED, WHERE WORRY WOULD FIT RIGHT IN.

HEAD TO TAKE A SHOWER, AND AS I'M GOING UP,

I SWITCH THE COFFEE IN MY HANDS AND FINISH UP THE CUP.

PUT IT ON THE DRESSER, EVENTUALLY SOON TO DRESS,

TAKE SOMETIME CLEANING UP, TO STRAIGHTEN ALL MY MESS.

GET MY COAT AND KEYS, NOW LOCK UP ALL THE DOORS,

NOW I'M AWAKE, TO FACE THE DAY, THANKFULLY ONCE MORE!

APOLOGIES

MISDIRECTED APLENTY, BEEN BLINDSIDED, LED ASKEW,

CAN'T COMPLETELY RECALL, ALL THE FOG, I'VE BEEN THRU.

HOW WONDERFUL ARE THE SIGHT LINES, BEFORE SOME EVERY DAY,

FOR MOST OF US, CHOICE HAS NO OPTION, AS WE GO ON OUR WAY.

THE LUCKY ONES ARE ALWAYS GUIDED, IN LIFE ALONG ITS PATH,

MOST OF US ARE FORCED TO WANDER, SEEKING HELP ON ONE'S BEHALF.

ADVICE, IT MAY BE PRUDENT, AND SINCERE WHEN IT IS SAID,

FACTS SOMETIMES ARE LACKING, WITH SOME CHALLENGES UP AHEAD.

AS AN HOURGLASS CALCULATES, FROM BEGINNING TO THE END,

THE TIMING IN LIFE IS FICKLE, AND FAR FROM BEING YOUR FRIEND.

COMMITMENTS ARE SOMETIMES BROKEN, NEED EXPLAINING TO ATTONE,

REGARDLESS OF THE CIRCUMSTANCE, YOU ARE NOT ALL ALONE.

THE CROWD INCLUDES THOSE MISFITS, THAT MIX WELL WITH THE SANE,

ATTEMPTS CAN BE QUITE ENDLESS WHEN DIVIDING UP THE BLAME.

UNQUALIFIED AS HURTFUL, BUT JUSTIFIED AS HURT,

NOT ABLE TO REALIZE, THE SITUATION TO AVERT.

JUST ONE BROKEN PROMISE, NEED TO OPEN UP THE GATE,

TO AN UNCONTROLLED WORLD, THAT COULD REGULATE YOUR FATE.

INGREDIENTS OF LIFE, REQUIRE SORRY AT LENGTH,

FOREVER WILL MEASURE YOUR MORALS, CHARACTER, AND STRENGTH.

A POETS VIEW ON POETRY

A LIFE CONSUMED IN POETRY HAS OCCUPIED MY TIME

MY THOUGHTS SUBMERGED, BECOME AFLOAT, FORMING INTO RHYME

THERE'S SOMETIMES A TRACE OF AGONY WHEN FORCING TO CREATE

OFTEN PANIC, WHERE'S YOUR PEN, THESE MOMENTS WILL NOT WAIT

SUBSTANCE WON'T BE HARNESSED, RESERVED, OR IN THE WINGS,

CAUTION IN ITS APPEARANCE, SUBDUED IN WHAT IT BRINGS

IDEAS SOMETIMES EXPLODING, NO PEN CAN MATCH THEIR PACE,

ACCOUNTING FOR EVERY DETAIL MADE, A LITERARY RACE

IT HASTENS AT ITS OWN SPEED, BEHOLDING TO NO GAUGE,

IT SPARKLES WITH A GLISTENING SHIELD, ATTACKING PERHAPS IN RAGE.

THE BALANCE OF ALL WORDING THRIVES BEST IN UNCONTROL,

ALWAYS GETS ACCEPTANCE, NO MATTER WHAT THE ROLE

A SMELL, THE SIGHTS, THE WHITE NOISE, WILL ENTER IN THE MIX,

RECONSTRUCTION, CONSTANT CHANGES, AND EVENTUALLY THE FIX

WHEN ALL IS SAID AND WRITTEN, ACCEPTED BY THE PEN,

ADJUSTMENT LIKELY TO INTRUDE, ALWAYS CHANCE YOU START AGAIN

CITY ON THE OCEAN
(THE BOARDWALK)

THAT ALL TOO FAMILIAR FIRM BOARDWALK CORE,

THE FERRIS WHEEL, JILLY'S, THE SEAGULLS, AND THE SHORE.

BIZZARE SUMMER OUTFITS, OUTDONE MORE EACH YEAR,

ADMIRING THE CHARACTERS, THAT DISPLAY WITHOUT FEAR.

THE PIRATE WAS ALL SO DAPPER, WITH HIS SWORD AND BRIGHT RED SASH,

ADVERTISING PIRATE COVE, TO THE CROWDS THAT NOW AMASS.

A NIGHT FULL OF CARRIAGES, WITH NEWBORNS AROUND GALORE,

WHOSE PARENTS HAD THEIR PARENTS, PUSH THEM HERE BEFORE?

ENDLESS IS THE BEAUTY, THE COLORS, AND THE SIGHTS,

SUNGLASSES IN THE NIGHTTIME, ENHANCING THE DELIGHTS.

APPEARING NOW BEFORE ME, THE BOARDWALKS ENDLESS PATH,

ABUSED WITH MANY FOOTSTEPS, AND ALL DAY WITH OUR WRATH.

IT FLEXES WITH THUNDER, THE SOUNDS THROUGHOUT THE BOARDS,

SUSTAINS THE CONSTANT MOVEMENTS, FROM THE FOOTWEAR OF THE HOARDS.

PROVIDING PURPOSE EVERY DAY, ENCOURAGING A WALK,

FOR GATHERING THOUGHTS, PEACE OF MIND, COFFEE, AND EVEN TALK.

THE SURFACES ALL ENCOUNTER, ALL MUSIC AND THE NOISE,

FOOD IS DROPPING, FEET ARE STOMPING, ABSORBING WHAT DEPLOYS.

THE PEOPLE AND THEIR RHYTHMS, THEIR MOTIONS KEEPING TIME,

THE MOVING CROWDS ARE ENDLESS, NEVER IN DECLINE.

WHAT'S TO BE SAID, HOW MANY DESCRIPTIONS, THAT FURTHER COULD ALIGN,

ANOTHER WAY OF CHANGING, WHAT ALREADY IS SUBLIME.

WILL ALL OUR MANY QUESTIONS, HAVE ANSWERS AND AMENDS,

WHERE WE JUSTIFY VACATION, THE WEEK MADE OF PRETEND.

CHALLENGER

(1-28-88)

NOW ONE YEAR LATER, STILL UNHEALED SORROW ON THE GROUND,

MY DEEP EMOTIONS LINGER, AND MY HEART IT YET SURROUNDS.

BY THE LOSS OF OUR BROTHERS, AND OUR SISTERS OUT IN SPACE,

TO A NEW WORLD, AND BEYOND, LOST IN TIME AND PLACE.

PIONEERS ONE AND ALL, WE HAIL WITH SACAGAWEA, LEWIS AND CLARK,

DISPLAYING COURAGE AND HUMILITY, IN PREPARATION TO EMBARK.

WE ADMIRE THEIR GREATNESS, LONG WILL MOURN THEIR LOSS IN FLIGHT,

WE'RE STRONG TO HOLD IN MEMORY, IMMORTAL IS THEIR LIGHT,

ETERNAL THEIR MISSION, THE HEAVENS ALWAYS THEIR GRAIL,

THEY MOVED TOWARD THE UNKNOWN, ON TIME, WITHOUT FAIL.

LIKE THE WAVES OF OUR OCEANS, ENDLESS TO OUR SHORE,

THEIR SACRIFICE TO MANKIND, LIVES ON FOREVER MORE.

CHRISTMAS STORY'S

BEGINS WITH THAT CHANNEL, OF LIFE ON TV,

THOUGHTS START TO GROW AND AWAKEN IN ME.

NOW AWARE OF THE COUNTDOWN, TOWARD THAT BIG DAY,

YOU RECOGNIZE IT'S CHRISTMAS TIME, AT THE BEGINNING OF MAY?

FROM THE MOMENT YOU WATCH, THEIR SHOWS IN THE SPRING,

THE WHEELS START TO SPIN, THOUGHTS OF PRESENTS TO BRING.

THERE'S THE STRUGGLE FOR A FAKE TREE, IT'S DEBATED MANY TIMES,

TO OFFER LESS MAINTENANCE, IN SAFETY AND DESIGN.

REUSEABLE AND LIFELIKE, IN A POSITION OF TRADITION,

LACK OF NATURE'S TREE SCENT, LESS NEED FOR CLEAN UP AMBITION.

THERE'S THE SECRET SANTA, CONFUSION AMPLIFIED,

PRESENTING GIFTS TO BE ACCEPTED, WITH OPTION, ARE DENIED.

TO GIVE ANOTHER CHANCE, TO YOUR NUMBER IN THE LINE,

YOU TAKE A CHANCE TO TRADE UP, YOUR GIFT PERCHANCE REFINE.

COMMUNICATION AND ERRANDS, WITH ME, SOON COLLIDE,

CONFUSING THE LOGISTICS, TO SATISFY ALL SIDES.

ACQUAINTANCES AND FRIENDS, NOT SO ANYMORE,

GIVE YOU SOME RELIEF, TO REDUCE YOUR GIFTING CHORE.

WHEN YOU END THE CELEBRATION AND ALL THAT IT INCLUDES,

ALL CEREMONY IS NOW OVER, AND POMP AND CIRCUMSTANCE CONCLUDE.

DAZED NOR CONFUSED

HOW HAS LIFE ESCAPED YOU, SO FREQUENTLY UNAWARE,

THE TRUTHS, THE FALSEHOODS, AND NEGATIVE ACTIONS, PROPELLING THE DESPAIR.

ARE YOU REALLY THAT UNHAPPY, WITH WHAT YOU HAVE RECEIVED,

WAS NOT WHAT YOU DESERVE NOR EARNED, BUT PROGRESSIVELY BELIEVED.

DUMBING DOWN, PURSUE WITH RIOTS, ENCOURAGING THE STORM,

DELUGE FROM THE MISINFORMED, DIRECTS US TO MORE HARM.

DESTROYING CITIZEN STRUCTURE, OUR CENTURIES OLD FORMED BASE,

FORSAKE THE CONSTITUTION, AND MORE TYRANNY IN ITS PLACE.

THERE'S NO "PROGRESS" IN "PROGRESSIVE", NO "AWAKENESS" IN THE "WOKE",

YOU SET THE WORLD ON FIRE AND LEGITIMIZE THE SMOKE.

DILEMMA

RETURNING FROM MY WALK,

DIRECT SUN IN MY EYES,

A HEADING POINTING WESTWARD,

BLURRED VISION NO SURPRISE.

CONCERNED THAT MY IDEAS,

MAY EXHAUST ME AS I WALK,

INSIDE I AM APPEASED,

AND SOON GIVE ME A TALK.

HOW NOT CAN YOU SEE TELLING,

OF VERSE, PROSE, AND RHYME,

IT APPEARS, AND THEN PURSUES YOU,

TO ARRANGE A POEM SUBLIME.

THEN CONTINUES TO GET KINDER,

ETERNAL IF IT'S SOUND,

FLOWS NORTH AND EAST, SOUTH, AND WEST,

WHEN WALKING HALLOWED GROUND.

FENCES FALLING DOWN

FENCES FALLING DOWN, EASING TO THE GROUND,

LEAVING JUST THE MEMORIES BEHIND.

THINGS THAT THEY KEPT IN, THINGS THAT MIGHT HAVE BEEN,

SWEPT AWAY BY FORCES, SOME UNKIND.

ROLLING GRASSES SWAYED, HORSES OFTEN PLAYED,

RUNNING LIKE THE WIND WHEN TIMES WERE GOOD,

TRAILERED FAR AWAY, SOMEWHERE ELSE THEY STAY,

THE REASONS THEY CAN'T STAY ARE UNDERSTOOD.

FENCES FALLING DOWN, PIECES ON THE GROUND,

LEFT STANDING NOW A SPACE FOR VISIONED FEW,

FENCES FALLING DOWN, LYING ON THE GROUND,

BROKEN PIECES ARE UNLIKELY, TO BE ASSEMBLED ANEW.

WE WILL COMPROMISE, KNOWING IT IS WISE,

THE OLD FENCE SERVED US WELL AS WE ALL KNOW,

PERHAPS WE BUILD AGAIN, A FORM OF COMPROMISE,

CONSTRUCT A FUTURE FENCE WE CAN BESTOW.

FOUR BOYS

THERE WERE FOUR BOYS,

AT EACH OTHER'S THROATS,

TOO MUCH NOISE, I DID WONDER,

HOW THE FAMILY COPED.

THE DRINKING THAT WENT ON,

IN THE DAY, AND AT NIGHT.

THERE WAS SPEEDING, NOT A SIGN,

OF SLOWING DOWN IN SIGHT.

"I KNOW WHAT I'M DOING, JUST LEAVE ME ALONE."

"YOU CAN'T MAKE ME DO THAT; MY LIFE IS MY OWN"

PURPOSE REMOTE, LIFE WAS TOO FAST,

NO RESTRICTIONS, UNCONFINED,

WITH NO THOUGHT IT WOULD LAST.

NOW THERE WERE THREE BOYS, QUITE A RESULT,

ALL ARE STILL IN THE FAST LANE, DESTINED TO MELT.

LOVE WAS ELUSIVE, DREAMS CAME AND WENT,

DRINKING WAS RAMPANT, AND ANOTHER LIFE WAS SPENT.

THEN THERE WERE TWO BOYS, NOT MUCH HAD CHANGED,

DRINKING WAS HEAVY, RAGE STILL ENGAGED.

WHY DID IT HAPPEN, REALITY SET IN,

THINGS FELL AND STUMBLED, FROM WHAT COULD HAVE
BEEN.

"I KNOW WHAT I'M DOING, JUST LEAVE ME ALONE",

"YOU CAN'T MAKE ME DO THAT; MY LIFE IS MY OWN".

THEN THERE WAS ONE BOY, TO CARRY THE GUILT,

IT CONTINUED TO PLAGUE HIM, THE PAIN THAT HE FELT,

ONCE THERE WERE FOUR BOYS, NOW THERE IS NONE,

"I KNOW WHAT I'M DOING, JUST LEAVE ME ALONE,

"YOU CAN'T MAKE ME DO THAT; MY LIFE IS MY OWN".

FRIENDS AND ENEMIES

FRIENDS MAY LEAD TO ENEMIES, SOME ENEMIES LEAD TO FRIENDS,

MY ENEMIES ENEMY, IS MY ALLY, THE ROAD NOW TWISTS AND BENDS.

WITH GOOD THOUGHT AND TRUST IN HEART, WE LEAP TO BUILD A WAY,

TOWARD HELPING OTHERS, SHARING WISDOM, AND CONTRIBUTING TO LIFE ARRAY.

DEFLECT MISTAKES TOGETHER, REBUILD A STRONGER WALL,

ENCOURAGE A CLEARER PATHWAY, THUS PREVENTING A FUTURE FALL.

SHARE EACH OTHER'S BOUNTY, SHARE THE TIMES WHEN TOUGH,

REALIZE WITH UNDERSTANDING, THERE NEVER IS ENOUGH.

FRIENDS UNIQUE CAN BE PARTNERS, BUT UTMOST STAND-ALONE,

DEVELOPING THEIR OWN WAY, BUILDING VALUES NOT YET KNOWN.

WHEN CONFLICT OF OPINION, BECOMES "THE MOUSE THAT ROARS",

OUR "MIDDLE GROUND" STARTS TO SHRINK, AND AGREEMENT WILL CLOSE THE DOOR.

TO OVERCOME EACH BATTLE, NEEDS THE PROPHET, COMPROMISE,

ALONE WE PONDER, IT'S WHAT WE DO, IT'S HEALTHY, RIGHT, AND WISE.

TO CHANGE AN ENEMY TO A FRIEND, IS ONE OF LIFES REWARDS,

BUT CHANGING A FRIEND TO ONE'S ENEMY SHOULD BE A LAST RESORT.

HOME SCHOOLING
(NO WOKE)

THE CONTENT OF MY CHARACTER, HAS COLORED UP MY SKIN,

I'M CURRENTLY AVOIDING DRAMA, THAT I COULD GET IN.

YOU TELL ME ALL MY DECISIONS, SURELY MUST BE WRONG,

THE RULES APPLIED JUST YESTERDAY, YOU JUST CAN'T GO ALONG.

I'M GOING WITH THE BASICS OF LIFE, TRUE TO MYSELF, NOT ALWAYS RIGHT.

I'M GONNA KEEP ON LIVING MY LIFE, BE PROUD OF MYSELF, AND ENCOURAGE MY FIGHT.

IT'S PRETTY SIMPLE, YES, I'M SIMPLE, YEAH SIMPLE KEEPS ME FREE,

SIMPLE, YEAH REAL SIMPLE, IT ALWAYS WORKED FOR ME.

ATTENTION TO "WOKE NATION", THERE'S NO "WOKE" IN YOUR AWAKE,

YOU HAVE NO PROGRESS IN "PROGRESSIVE", YOUR HISTORY REEKS MISTAKE.

HOMETOWN ROAD OF LIFE

THE ROAD I'M ON TODAY, ITS STRUCTURED WITH MANY MOVES,

PARALLELS THE NEARBY STREAM, MANEUVERS WITH ITS CURVES.

SUTTLE GRADES OF UPS AND DOWNS, PORTRAY ITS MAGIC SCENE,

THAT FLOWS WITH PLANTS, AND STONES, AND LEAVES, BLENDING IN BETWEEN.

OCCASIONALLY IT STRAIGHTENS, WITH VIEWS BOTH BLUE AND CLEAR,

QUICKLY TURNING AT ITS UPHILL END, DOWNHILL EFFORTS NEAR.

INCIDENT UNCOMMON, MANY THOUGHTS HAVE RULED THIS TIME,

ENCOUNTERS OF KIND SILENCE, PERSERVERING SO SUBLIME.

HOW WILL THOU REMEMBER THEE

ONE THOUGHT THAT OFTEN COMES TO ME,

WHAT PATH WILL FORM MY LEGACY?

DIRECTION SO SCATTERED AND FRACTURED BY FATE,

ON TIME FOR MANY DEEDS, AND EQUALY SOME LATE.

SO YOUNG AND NOT KNOWING, THE IMPORTANCE OF TIME,

MY CLOCK-TICKING YOUTH, WAS REALLY NOT MINE.

IT BELONGED TO A CULTURE, A FAMILY SO LOST,

MAINTAINING AN EXISTENCE, REFUSING ITS COST.

OUR SO MANY BRIDGES, WERE BURNED ON THE WAY,

THE RESULTS OF THESE CHOICES, STILL LINGER TODAY.

AS CHILDREN WE FOLLOWED, TO TRUST RIGHT AND WRONG,

IN LINE WITH THE RESOURCE, TO BRING US ALONG.

ATTACHED TO OUR MENTORS, OUR GUIDES IN THE STORM,

STEERING LIFE UNCERTAIN, TO MINIMIZE THE HARM.

OPPORTUNITY FOR IMPRESSION, WAS RECOGNIZED AS FLEET,

THE ACCEPTANCE OF SUGGESTIONS, ON OCCASION DISCREET.

MOVING STILL FORWARD, AS THE LESSONS ARE SENT,

NOT ALL OF THEM ARE COMFORTABLE, SOME LEAD TO RESENT.

THE RESULTS OF POOR JUDGEMENTS WOULD SOON COME TO REST,

WHILE THE ROUTES OF OPINION, CAME QUICKLY TO SUGGEST.

TAKEN ADVICE, DEMONSTRATIONS OBSERVED,

GOES ETERNAL THROUGH LIFE, TO PROGRESS ON A CURVE.

SO FAMILIAR WITH STRUGGLE, BUT LEARNING TO COPE,

EVENTUAL RECOGNITION, NEW AVENUES OF HOPE.

THOSE SIGNALS OF TRUST, THE ABSORPTION OF TRUTH,

TO SORT OUT THE CLUTTER, ESTABLISHED IN YOUTH.

A LONG PAINFUL ROAD, SOMETIMES DARK AND UNSURE,

WILL SOON BRING THE LIGHT, UNANNOUNCED IN A BLUR.

OFTEN THE CLICHÉ "TAKE A DAY AT A TIME"

ADVICE THROUGH THE AGES, NO NEED TO REFINE.

ALIVE WITH FRUSTRATION WHAT TO WRITE ON OUR STONE,

BELONGS TO THE LIVING TO WRITE WHEN I'M GONE.

,

HUNTING CABIN FRENCH TOAST

1 LOAF OF BREAD (UNSLICED FOR PREFERRED THICKNESS)

1 CUP OF MILK

1 EGG

¼ LB. OF BUTTER

1 SHALLOW DISH MIXING BOWL

1 FORK

1 BLACK IRON SKILLET

1 SPATULA

1 BOTTLE OF SKINNER MOUNTIAN HOMEMADE MAPLE SYRUP

DIRECTIONS:

USE THE FORK, TO WHIP THE EGG AND THE MILK TOGETHER IN THE SHALLOW BOWL TO A FOAMY, WELL-MIXED TEXTURE.

PLACE THE SKILLET ON MEDIUM HEAT.

PLACE A PAT OF BUTTER IN THE PAN AND DISTRIBUTE IT EVENLY ON THE SURFACE

DIP ONE BREAD SLICE AT A TIME EVENLY ON BOTH SIDES INTO THE BOWL MIXTURE.

PUT THE PREPARED SLICES ONTO THE SKILLET SURFACE. (3 SLICES)

WITH THE FLIPPER, LIFT THE SLICES TO CHECK ON THEIR GOAL OF GOLDEN BROWN

FLIP SLICES TO THEIR OTHER SIDE

CONTINUE UNTIL BOTH SIDES AND THE MIDDLE OF THE TOAST ARE DONE TO YOUR PREFERENCE.

SERVE WITH MELTED BUTTER AND SKINNER MOUNTIAN HOMEMADE MAPLE SYRUP

I AM THE HOMELESS

WHAT'S IT BEEN LIKE THIS TIME, LIVING ALONE,

TRYING TO SHARE MY FEELINGS.

I COME ACROSS THE STRANGEST THINGS, EVERYWHERE I TURN,

LOOKING TO FIND OUT SOME ANSWERS.

I AM THE HOMELESS, LOOKING FOR A PLACE TO STAY,

BUT I CAN'T SEEM TO FIND A WARM SPACE.

WIND BLOWING MY HAIR, I'M FIGHTING THIS COLD,

CARDBOARD AND RAGS, COVER UP MY FACE.

I LIVE IN YOUR PARKS, UNDER A BOX,

ANYWHERE OPEN, I CAN FIND SHELTER.

I TRIED LIVING IN YOUR SPACE, TOO MANY RULES,

I'D RATHER CONFRONT, ALL THE DANGERS.

WHY DO I DO WHAT I DO, IT'S OF MY OWN CHOICE,

TOO MANY TIMES, MY BACK BEEN AGAINST THE WALL.

AS LONG AS I DRINK, AND DRESS MYSELF WARM,

I CAN COLLECT CANS AND MAKE IT THROUGH IT ALL.

PEOPLE TALKING, BUT I'M NOT LISTENING,

THEY THINK THEY KNOW ME, BUT I'M NOT HEARING,

IF THEY TOOK THE TIME, TO LOOK DEEP INTO MY EYES,

THEY'D SEE THE REAL ME, AND THEY COULD VISUALIZE.

AND SEE THE REAL ME, AND UNDERSTAND MY PAIN,

AND MAYBE HEAL ME, SO I COULD REBUILD AGAIN.

IT ENDS WITH THIS BOTTLE, MUCH LIKE IT STARTS,

LIKELY PERMANENT PAINT IN MY CORNER,

I'M COUNTING ON SUMMER, TO GET HERE REAL FAST,

MY SPIRITS ARE UP WHEN I'M WARMER.

I CAN'T SEEM TO STOP IT, THIS PATH THAT I'M ON,

WHERE WILL I BE TOMORROW?

I'LL TRY TO MAKE IT, OVER ONE MORE HILL, AND WHEN I'M ON TOP,

I'LL CHECK OUT THE WIDE AND NARROW.

PEOPLE TALKING, BUT I'M NOT LISTENING,

THEY THINK THEY KNOW ME, BUT I'M NOT HEARING,

IF THEY TOOK THE TIME, TO LOOK DEEP INTO MY EYES,

THEY'D SEE THE REAL ME, AND THEY COULD VISUALIZE,

AND SEE THE REAL ME, AND UNDERSTAND MY PAIN,

AND MAYBE HEAL ME, SO I COULD REBUILD AGAIN.

JUST LAST NIGHT
(9/11/01)

LAST NIGHT, WE HAD A FIGHT

WHO WAS WRONG, AND WHO WAS RIGHT.

LAST NIGHT, WE HAD A FIGHT,

WE NEVER KISSED TO SAY GOODNIGHT.

UP EARLY THIS MORNING, COULD ONLY SEE YOUR SHADOW,

THEN MOVING TOWARD THE DOOR, IN A PEACEFUL WAY,

I DON'T NEED THE LIGHT, TO KNOW WHAT I KNOW,

YOUR EVERY MOVE IS KNOWN, BECAUSE IT'S DAY AFTER DAY.

AFTER YOUR SHORT SHOWER, IN UNIFORM YOU'LL DRESS,

CLOSE IS THE TIME YOU HAVE TO GO; I WAIT FOR YOUR CARESS.

I'M HOPING YOU'LL HOLD ME, LET YOUR FEELINGS SHOW,

BUT YOU LEFT WITHOUT A WORD, AND NOW I'LL NEVER KNOW.

ON OUR LAST NIGHT, WE HAD A FIGHT,

NOW YOU'RE GONE IN THE ETERNAL LIGHT.

LAST NIGHT WE HAD OUR LAST FIGHT,

IT WILL NEVER MATTER WHO WAS WRONG OR RIGHT.

I WOULD GIVE ANYTHING RIGHT NOW, JUST TO BE WITH YOU,

TO TELL YOU THAT I DIDN'T MEAN IT.

AND IF WE HAD THE CHANCE, TO FACE IT ALL AGAIN,

IT REALLY MADE NO SENSE, WE SHOULD HAVE SEEN IT.

THAT LAST NIGHT, WE SURE HAD A FIGHT,

NEVER MATTERED, WHO WAS WRONG OR RIGHT.

EVERY NIGHT I'LL REMEMBER THAT FIGHT,

NO ONE'S TO BLAME FOR WHO'S WRONG OR RIGHT.

JUST SAYIN'

AWAKEN TO A RED SKY, BLUE ENTRAILS WHISPERED IN,

A LARGE BLACK CLOUD SLIPPED INTO VIEW; THE DAY
WOULD NOW BEGIN.

OFTEN AS I AWAKEN, UPSET THAT I AM TOO LATE,

RECOGNIZING TIME AND SPEED, ARE STRUCTURES OF MY
FATE.

MANY PEOPLE I HAVE KNOWN, SOME SEALED
UNDERGROUND,

OTHERS ARE THROWN OUT, TO THE WIND; SOME JUST CAN'T
BE FOUND.

KNOWING OF THE BALANCE, IN LIFE THAT WE ALL SHARE,

MORE THAN SIMPLY RIGHTS, OR WRONGS, AND LOVE AND
HOPE AND CARE.

AWARE OF THE OPPORTUNITY TO RECOGNIZE THE TRUTH,

ALWAYS TAKING LEAPS OF FAITH, MAINTAINING PARTS OF
YOUTH.

WE'RE WARY OF POSTPONEMENT, AS WE OFTEN LINGER
THERE,

FRUITLESS TO IGNORE ITS PRESENCE, IMPORTANT TO BE
AWARE.

ALL KNOWING WITH MODERATION, FOR OUR
STEPPINGSTONES IN LIFE,

DON'T OVERTHINK YOUR HISTORY, YOUR RECORDED
WRONGS OR RIGHTS.

MY GOAL IS TO AWAKEN, TAKE DEEP BREATHS WHILE I CAN,

TO SAVOR WHAT'S BEFORE ME, TO FORMULATE NEW PLANS.

ALTHOUGH RESOURCE HAS BEEN REDUCED, OPTIONS WILL GET FEW,

WE MUST ACCEPT, IF WE AWAKEN, EACH DAY WILL BE BRAND NEW.

LABOR DAY WEEKEND

YOUR WORKDAY IS OVER BEFORE IT HAS BEGUN,

ALL ENERGY IS NOW FOCUSED, ON THE TRAVEL AND SOME FUN.

THE TRUNKS ALL NEED PACKING, LOGISTICS MUST BE KEEN.

TIME NOW TAKES OVER, A DESERVING CHANGE OF SCENE.

YOU WORK OUT DIRECTIONS, SOMETIMES IT'S THE SAME,

SOME PLACES ARE COMMON, SOME WITH A DIFFERENT NAME.

A BOAT IS YOUR PLEASURE, PERHAPS THE RARE CUISINE,

DULL MOMENTS ARE OBSCURE, SOME SLEEP CAUGHT INBETWEEN.

YOUR BUDGET PLAN IS ABSENT, TO YOUR INTEREST AND DELIGHT,

THE GOAL, TAKE ADVANTAGE, OF THE DAY AND THE NIGHT

PARTICIPATE FREELY, SEEKING FUN AT ALL COSTS,

EXPECT TIME HAS LIMITS, YOU'RE PROTECTING IT FROM LOSS.

AS SIGNS OF ITS ENDING, FORM SLOWLY WITH EACH DAY,

ADJUSTMENTS ARE MADE, FOR CLOSURE ON THE WAY.

SECURING NEW MEMORIES, TO SHARE WITH NEW FRIENDS,

IN A VAULT OF YOUR FEELINGS, WHERE LABOR DAY NEVER ENDS.

LES' JOY
[THE LAMENT OF LESTER]

WE CAN ONLY LIVE OUR LIVES, THE BEST THAT WE KNOW HOW,

TRUST OUR FAMILY, FRIENDS, AND GOD, WITH WHAT THEY WILL ALLOW.

TO STAY WITHIN THE LINES, WHEN WE COLOR IN OUR BOOK,

KEEP IN MIND THE GOLDEN RULE, WHEN WE'RE MISUNDERSTOOD.

WE FACE THE STRUGGLE EVERYDAY, ONE MOMENT TO THE NEXT,

AND AT DAYS END, WE DO SURVIVE, AND KNOW THAT WE ARE BLESSED.

FAMILIES SHARE THEIR UPSETS, BROTHER, SISTER SHARE THE PAIN,

ON GOOD DAYS WE AWAKEN TO FACE LIFE ONCE AGAIN.

OUR JOURNEY ON THIS EARTH IS CHANGING EVERYDAY,

THIS ROAD OF LIFE HAS ENDED, COME LAY DOWN.

WE MUST RECALL WHAT WE HAVE LEARNED, ABOUT GOD'S PLAN FOR US,

OUR JOYOUS SOUL AND SPIRIT, HE LEADS TO HIGHER GROUND.

CARE FOR US, FOR AT THIS TIME, WE'RE LOST AND SO AFRAID,

GIVE US HOPE, YOU KNOW WE WAIT, TO HEAR WHAT GOD HAS SAID.

IN LIFETIME, OVER LIFETIME, WE'RE BORN INTO GOD'S REIGN,

WE STRUGGLE WITH OUR HEART AND SOUL, TO RETURN TO HIM AGAIN.

SO FRAGILE WHEN WE'RE BORN, AND MUCH SO WHEN WE DIE,

THE MORE THINGS CHANGE, THE MORE THEY REMAIN THE SAME,

IN LIFETIME OVER LIFETIME, WE'RE BORN INTO YOUR REIGN,

TO STRUGGLE WITH THAT HEART AND SOUL, TO RETURN TO YOU AGAIN.

THIS JOURNEY ON THIS EARTH IS CHANGING ON THIS DAY,

THIS ROAD OF LIFE HAS ENDED, COME LAY DOWN.

WE MUST RECALL WHAT WE HAVE LEARNED, ABOUT GOD'S PLAN FOR US.

OUR SOUL AND JOYOUS SPIRIT, HE LEADS TO HIGHER GROUND.

OUR SOUL AND JOYOUS SPIRIT, HE LEADS TO HIGHER GROUND.

LOVE HURTS

I WILL LOVE YOU UNTIL THE END OF TIME.

I WILL LOVE YOU UNTIL THE END OF

I WILL LOVE YOU UNTIL THE END

I WILL LOVE YOU UNTIL THE

I WILL LOVE YOU UNTIL

I WILL LOVE YOU

I WILL LOVE

I WILL

I

I GAVE AND YOU TOOK

I GAVE AND YOU

I GAVE AND

I GAVE

I

I THINK LOVE IS OVERRATED

I THINK LOVE IS

I THINK LOVE

I THINK

I

P.S.

OUR LOVE WILL LAST FOREVER

YOU COMPLETE ME, AND MAKE ME WHOLE

MISTAKES ARE HEALTHY

ON OCCASION, I'VE KNOWN MANY THINGS, OFTEN BEEN PUT ON THE SPOT,

SELF-RESOURCE WILL KEEP ME GOING, AT THE TIME IS WHAT I THOUGHT.

OVERRATING WHAT YOU KNOW, HAS PROBLEMS DOWN THE ROAD,

COMPLICATIONS HINDER PROGRESS, WE HAVE OFTEN ALL BEEN TOLD.

MOST KNOWLEDGE I HAVE GATHERED, WAS LEARNED BECAUSE I FAILED,

THIS MAIN LESSON IN ITSELF, PROVIDES REASON THAT I PREVAILED.

REPETITION IN LESSONS IS HEALTHY, REDUCING THE CHANCE OF MISSING THE MARK,

ACCEPTING REWORK, KEEPS THE DISTANCE, FROM MOVING INTO WHAT'S DARK.

WHEN ATTEMPTING A GOAL FOR THE FIRST TIME, ENCOURAGE OPINION IN THE MIX,

THE SHARING OF PLANNING IS HEALTHY AND WILL HELP EXPEDITE THE FIX.

RECONSTRUCTION IN YOUR METHODS MAY CREATE SOME COLLATERAL DAMAGE,

OVER TIME YOU GAIN ON CLOSURE, TO ASSURE A LIMIT TO YOUR BAGGAGE.

WHO'S TO SAY, WHICH PATHS ARE STRAIGHT, IF WE CAN'T SEE WHERE IT ENDS,

HEADINGS ALWAYS INCLUDE SOME TURNS, SOMETIMES SUBTLE, IN THE BENDS.

CHOSEN SCHEDULES PRESENT A FOREPLAY, IN THE
PLANNING OF OUR LIFE,

OPPORTUNITY WITH ITS WINDOW, HAS FIRST-TIME LIMITS
TO GET IT RIGHT.

MY BALLAD OF THE MAILMAN SAM FREE

TWELVE IN '59, OUR NATIONAL PAST TIME WAS MY LOVE,

SOME SUMMER DAYS AT 3 O'CLOCK, RAN UPTOWN WITH MY GLOVE.

I'D CATCH MY RIDE WITH THE MAILMAN, THE RIDE TO TAKE ME HOME,

SOME DAYS, YOU WERE HIS SIDEKICK, BECAUSE THE MAILMAN RODE ALONE.

HE'D TAKE A RIDER IF HE KNEW YOU IF YOU TIMELY HAPPENED ROUND,

HE PICKED UP THE MAIL FROM THE RAILROAD STATION AND RETURNED IT BACK TO TOWN.

THEN 3:30 ON DOWN THE MOUNTAIN, A SHORT RIDE, SAY THREE MILES,

ALWAYS TALKING, ASKING QUESTIONS, SUCH ADVENTURE FILLED WITH SMILES.

HIS DESOTO WAS A MAGIC CAR, HIS OWN VEHICLE IN THOSE DAYS,

ALLOWED TO TRANSFER MAIL AND PARCELS, ON THEIR ADDRESSED WAYS.

EVERYDAY LIKE CLOCKWORK, AT NINE O'CLOCK AND THREE,

THE ENTIRE LOCAL GENTRY, KNEW EXACTLY WHERE HE'D BE.

MANY YEARS HAVE PASSED NOW, YET MEMORIES SO SINCERE,

SUBDUED THE IMPORTANCE OF THIS MAILMAN, HIS CHARACTER STILL HELD CLEAR.

SON OF A SLAVE, EVERYWHERE, FRAMED HIS PLACE, HIS MIND,

IT NEVER SURFACED ON HIS SLEEVE, HE WAS GENTLE AND TRULY KIND.

I LEARNED OF HIS PASSING, LEARNED MORE ABOUT HIS LIFE,

HE WAS THE BEST MAN WHEN MY GRANDPA, MADE GRANDMA HIS WIFE.

THEY WORKED YEARS TOGETHER, AT TIMES SIDE BY SIDE,

THEN WENT ON THEIR SEPARATE WAY, WHEN THE TIME WOULD ARRIVE.

IN WINTER SAM CUT ICE, WHEN IT THICKENED, ON THE POND,

HE ONCE FOUND A DROWNED MAN, BELOW THE ICE, IN THE MUD.

AS I READ THROUGH HIS OBIT, MARRIED SWEET, FOR EIGHTY YEARS,

RAISED PIGS, GOATS, AND CHICKENS, A FARMER NOW APPEARED.

I'M SURE HIS ANSWERS, TO MY QUESTIONS, COULD I ASK HIM THINGS NOW,

HE'D PROBABLY ANSWER ALMOST ANYTHING, THAT HIS TIME WOULD ALLOW.

SAM MANEUVERED THROUGH HIS LIFE, A HUNDRED YEARS AND MORE,

THE PRESIDENT'S LETTER, GAUGED SAMUEL'S WORTH, FAR BEYOND FIVE SCORE.

GENTLEMAN, GUIDE, MENTOR, AND FRIEND, FORMED SUCH HISTORY,

I HAVE LIFELONG ADMIRATION, FOR OUR MAILMAN SAMUEL FREE.

MY FRIENDS

AS BOYS WE WERE A SHOUT AWAY, HARDLY OUT OF SIGHT,

CONNECTED BY THE NEIGHBORHOOD, PRESENT DAY AND NIGHT.

EACH ONE OF US HAD LAWNS TO MOW, THE CHORES BEYOND BELIEF,

SOMEHOW FINISHED, MADE OUR ESCAPE, ADVENTURE WAS OUR RELIEF.

BASEBALL GOT OUR ATTENTION, BASKETBALL WAS OUR PRIME,

OCCASIONALLY A TREE FORT, WE ALWAYS MADE THE TIME.

PRACTICES FILLED UP OUR YOUTH, FOOTBALL, BASEBALL, TRACK,

WE RODE THE SCHOOL BUS TO START THOSE DAYS, WITH NO WAY TO GET BACK.

EXPERIENCES BUILD YOUR CHARACTER, SO OFTEN WE WERE TOLD,

BUT DURING MOMENTS AS YOU BUILD, EXPERIENCE SOMETIMES GETS OLD.

HITCH-HIKING, NOW FORBIDDEN, NEVER FOR THE FAINT OF HEART,

FEARLESS ATTEMPTS IN DAYLIGHT, HAPPY YOUR HOME BY DARK.

OUR FEATS OF ENGINEERING, DISPLAYED TENACIOUS WRATH,

SOFTBALL BACKSTOP, HOCKEY RINK, THEN STICKBALL CROSSED OUR PATH.

OUR LIVES CONTINUED TO CHANGE, WITH SERVICE, SCHOOL, AND LOVE.

THERE ARE CHILDREN, WORK, AND TRAVELING, TO FIT OUR SOCIAL GLOVE.

FORTUNE HAS BEEN GOOD TO US, SOUND MIND TO COMPREHEND,

ACCOMPLISHED MEMORIES ARE STILL EXCHANGED, WITH PARTNERS I CALL FRIENDS.

MY MARKERS

SOMEWHAT YOU MUST RECALL, THOSE MARKERS IN YOUR LIFE,

THE RAILS, THE TIES, AND THE WATER, ALWAYS PAINT YOUR SIGHT.

THE GRASSY FIELD, THOSE BLACKTOP COURTS, ARE EVERY YOUNG BOY'S VIEW,

IT'S HOW WE SHAPE THOSE MEMORIES, THAT GUIDE THE WAY FOR YOU.

RAILS AND TIES, MAKE WAY FOR PATHS, ENDLESS IN LIFE'S SCENES,

TO RUN AND WALK, AND STOP FOR THOUGHT, ON PATHS TO UNKNOWN DREAMS.

THE COURTS THAT PAINT A SCHEME, OF RIGOR ON YOUR WAY,

NEVER REALIZED TILL YOU HAVE GROWN, THEY HELPED YOU TO THIS DAY.

GRASSY FIELDS, DIAGRAMED, RIDGID, AND SO STERN,

FILLED WITH RULES, WOOD BATS, AND SPHERES, TO MARK YOUR EVERY TURN.

THE STREAMS, THE PONDS, PINEKILL NEARBY, TAKE PART IN LIFE EACH DAY,

WITH BRIDGE ADVENTURES, SPORT, AND FEAR, LIFE MARKERS ARE ON DISPLAY.

MYSTIC CHORDS OF MEMORY

WAS EVER A FIGURE, SO REGAL, SO KIND,

THIS OVERWHELMING IMPRESSION, WAS FIRM IN MY MIND.

LED SO MANY OTHERS, MUCH LIKE MYSELF,

AS A YOUNG CHILD, FROM A BOOK ON THE SHELF.

READING BEGAN, OF A LIFE POOR AND PLAIN,

QUICKLY PIQUING MY INTEREST, MORE FACTS TO EXPLAIN.

KNOWLEDGE AND LEARNING, ARE MORE VALUED THAN GOLD,

OPENED UP THEATRE, FOR MY LIFE TO BEHOLD.

HIS STATURE WITH THE MASSES, STOOD OUT AMONG US ALL,

DEVELOPING A LEGEND, LETTING HISTORY INSTALL.

THE SACRIFICE, WORRY, THE SORROW, AND THE NERVE,

THE ELEGANT PROWESS, A MASTER WITH HIS WORDS.

OUR PUSHED HUMAN LIMITS, ALL CAUTION DISTURBED,

WOULD SOON OUTLIVE HIS EFFORTS, AND EXHAUST ALL RESERVES.

OUTPOURING THE SADNESS, SO DEEP IS THE WOUND,

NEVERENDING THE TERROR, UNBEARABLE THE SOUND.

SO STRONG HELD HIS SYMBOL, THE NAME FOREVER TO EXIST,

HIS POWER OF HEALING, ETERNAL WILL BE MISSED

THE FEVER OF DISCOURSE, TO THIS DAY, ALLOWED,

MY DEAR MR. LINCOLN, THE WORLD NEEDS YOU NOW.

NEW MORNING, NEW DAY

STILL NOT GRASPING, HOW TO GREET THE DAY,

SO EASY IN ACCEPTING, ANY PLANS TO DELAY,

A BLUR STILL CONSUMES, MY BODY, MY SPACE,

NOT YET CAN ACKNOWLEDGE, MY LOCATION, NOR PLACE.

SO SLOWLY MY LIMBS AND MY EYES FLOAT AWARE,

I DRAW SOME DEEP BREATHS, MY SIGHT MOIST IN STARE.

MANY THINGS ARE QUITE COMMON, AS I SLOWLY AWAKE,

ADMITTING THAT I KNOW, NEW DIRECTIONS I MAY TAKE.

THINKING ALL MY SENSES, HAVE FINALLY PREVAILED,

RECOGNIZING SOME PROGRESS CANNOT BE CURTAILED.

THINGS MOVING FORWARD, WHAT NOW SHOULD GET DONE,

REARRANGING THEIR ORDER, WORK NOW, AND OR FUN.

AWAKENING, CHANGING, AS THE DECADES BEGIN THEIR GLIDE,

FOR EVERYONE CAN BE DIFFERENT, IN HOW LIFE WILL PRESIDE.

IMPORTANCES NOT SO MUCH, ON PROGRESS YOU MAKE,

MORE SO ON OPPORTUNITIES, BEFORE LIFE ESCAPES.

WE MUST FIRST AWAKEN, TO REALIZE WE'VE DREAMED,

PROOF THAT WE ARE LIVING, MAINTAINING OUR LIFE SCHEME.

PARTICIPATE BOLDLY, WITH ADVENTURE AND CAUSE,

RECOGNIZE AN ADVANTAGE, LIFE NEVER DWELLS ON PAUSE.

OUR FOOTPRINTS IN THE SNOW

MY FOOTPRINTS AND YOUR PRINTS WILL NEVER BE THE SAME.

I CAN'T TELL YOUR COLOR; YOU DON'T KNOW MY NAME.

YOUR PRINT COVERS MY PRINT, AT TIMES IT SHOWS OUTSIDE,

DOES IT MEAN I LIKE BOUNDARIES, AS MY PRINT FITS INSIDE?

THERE ARE TIMES I WANDER FROM THE TRAIL, JUST TO BE ALONE,

LIKE OTHERS FURTHER DOWN, HIKE ELSEWHERE ON THEIR OWN.

OUR FOOTPRINTS WHEN TOGETHER ALWAYS WILL BE GOOD,

THOSE TIMES WHEN THEIR APART, REMAIN STILL UNDERSTOOD.

IF I STEP IN YOUR PRINTS, OR YOU COVER MINE,

OUR PURPOSE IS THE SAME, NEW DIRECTIONS WE MUST FIND.

THE MARKING OF OUR FOOTSTEPS, WE MARCH THE TRAIL ALL DAY,

DESTINATIONS MADE CLEAR AND SMOOTHER, FOR ALL FOLKS ON THE WAY.

COMFORTABLE DIRECTION NOW PROVEN TO BE TRUE,

BRINGING OUR NEW FOOTPRINTS, THEY'LL FOLLOW ME AND YOU.

POTHOLES IN THE SKY

THERE ARE POTHOLES IN THE SKY, LIMITLESS WE'RE TOLD,

MOTHER NATURE LIES BLEEDING, AND OUR INJUSTICES UNFOLD.

THE NATURAL WORLDS EXPLOITATION, AGAIN THEIR DECREE,

THE END POINT IS DESTRUCTION, INCREASED BY EACH DEGREE.

OBLITERATE COMBUSTION, FORBIDDEN, SOON IS LOST,

EXCELL YOUR NEW VERSIONS, ADVERSE TO ITS COST.

THE WHEEL TARIES WEARY, AT YOUR REINVENTION,

MISINFORMED LAWS OF NATURE, MISLEADING THE CONVENTION.

MODERATION AS RHETORIC, WILL IN TIME PREVAIL,

HELPING WITH THOSE POTHOLES, IN THE HEAVENS, WHERE THEY TRAIL.

RETIREMENT

I'M ALIVE, AND THAT'S GOOD, AND THERE'S A LOT TO BE SAID,

OF MAINTAINING A LIFESTYLE, THE DAILY RISING FROM BED.

PLANNING TIME WISELY, MAKE THE MOST OF YOUR LIFE,

EVERY MOMENT MAY CONFRONT YOU, WITH A HIGHIGHT OR STRIFE.

YOU DEVELOP NEW CHARACTERS, TO MEET SOME NEW GOALS,

CONSCIENCE OF FOOTING, AS NEW DIRECTIONS UNFOLD.

CAREFUL TO HOLD COURSE, WITH YOUR PRESENT THOUGHTOUT PLAN,

OPEN UP AND REFINE, OPPORTUNITY WHEN YOU CAN.

CONSTRUCTING SOME NEW SCHEDULE, MAY BE NEEDED AND USED,

FREE TIME ALWAYS PRECIOUS, AND CONVIENTLY ABUSED.

IN A PERFECT WORLD THERE'S GROWTH, ALWAYS MOVING AHEAD,

SOMETIMES IT'S BACKWARDS, YOU ENCOUNTER INSTEAD.

A NEW WORLD LIES OUT THERE, WITH DIFFERENCE AND QUESTION,

AN EVERYDAY SEARCH FOR ANSWERS, WILL BE BASED ON SUGGESTION.

YOUR ROLE OFTEN CHANGES, AND BLENDS WITH A TWIST,

WHAT'S FOUND ARE SOME ANSWERS, YOU SOMEHOW HAVE MISSED.

A RULE BOOK OF JUDGEMENT, MOSTLY MADE ON THE MOVE,

LEAVES MUCH TO CONSIDER, EVEN MORE NEEDS TO PROVE.

THE QUESTIONS OF FINANCE, LOGISTICS IN THE MIX,

REDUCED HELP FROM MENTORS, MAKE IT HARDER TO PREDICT

YOUR IN THEIR ROLE NOW, THE OLD GUARD IS GONE,

DECISIONS THAT EXTEND LIFE, NOW MADE ON YOUR OWN.

AGREEMENT WITH YOUR PARTNER, YOUR WIFE, OR A FRIEND,

MAKE THE BLEND OF EXISTENCE, MUCH EASIER TO EXTEND.

FOR NEVER ALL OF THE MYSTERIES, HAVE ANSWERS COMPLETE,

YOUR GOAL IS TO CHALLENGE AND MINIMIZE DEFEAT.

RHETORICAL NEWS

INFORMATION COLLECTED, SOON LACED WITH REVISION,

WHERE CHARACTERS UNWISE, ENACT UBIQUITOUS OPINIONS.

REPEATING THEIR STORIES, PROJECTED NEVER TO END,

WHILE SPRINKLING THE TRUTHS, WITH SOME LICENSE TO PRETEND.

POINTS OF VIEW ARE ABSTRACT, SOME MAY TOW THE LINE,

MOST MISS THE MARK, WITH THE SUBSTANCE THEY DEFINE.

THEY ENCIRCLE THEIR FOCUS, YET IT STILL GOES ASTRAY,

THEIR THOUGHTS, SELF-IMPORTANT, SUPPORTING DISARRAY.

COMPETING WITH OTHER PLATFORMS, SPINNING THROUGH THE DAY,

NARRATIVE REINFORCED, SO OFTEN FRIGHTENING THEIR PREY.

THEIR CATEGORIES ARE LISTLESS, DUMBED DOWN, AND POOR,

THE WEAK CAN'T SEE WHAT'S COMING, THROUGH THEIR FRONT DOOR.

AT LEAST SOME IMPORTANCE, STILL SUSTAINS WHEN WE DEBATE,

HOPE IN CHANGING THE LANDSCAPE, WITH THE POSSIBILITY OF GREAT.

WHEN THOSE WHO STRIKE THE MIDDLE, START TO INFECT,

AT LAST, SOME LIGHT ENTERS, REARRANGING THE EFFECT.

SHORT-LIVED, ABRUPT, BUT STILL BRINGING RELIEF,

ENCOURAGING WITH HOPE, TO MAINTAIN SOME BELIEF.

75 TODAY AND COUNTING

MY MOVEMENT BEATS ANOTHER DRUM, SOMEWAYS DIFFERENT, BUT THE SAME,

THE TREK MORE SIDEWAYS, THAN STRAIGHT AHEAD, ON POINT WITH TIME THAT STILL REMAINS,

MAINTAIN THE FRIENDSHIPS THAT I PROLONGED, RESPECT FOR ACCEPTANCE TO SECURE WHAT BELONGED,

SORTING THROUGH MY LIFETIME OF TEST RUNS, THAT TOOK THE BULK OF THE BRUNT ALL MY LIFE,

MADE SMART ENOUGH TO RECOGNIZE, WHAT TESTING COMPLETED WAS RIGHT.

FUNNY BUT IN THE BEGINNING, THE PAST WAS THEN THE MAIN FOCUS,

NOW MOVING ON, AS WE GET OLDER, CONCENTRATING ON "NOW", HAS APPROACHED US.

SETTLING DOWN, WORKING YOUR PLAN, YOUR CLOSER AND CLOSER EACH DAY,

OVERCOME THE CLOSED DOORS, MAYBE SOME SIDETRACKS, SURRENDER SOME BATTLES ON THE WAY.

WORK THROUGH ALL THE MYSTERIES, THE UNDEFINED DIRECTIONS,

YOUR PRECIOUS MENTAL HEALTH PROTECTED, ENFORCED BY YOUR SELECTIONS.

WANDER MANY TIMES AND MORE, ABSORBING WHAT IS FOUND,

REPEL THE WEEDS, AND THE STORMY SEAS, AND NEGATIVES THAT SURROUND.

NOW LOOKING AT THE HORIZONS, APPEARING TO REDEEM,

SPEND SOME GLADNESS, SEAS ARE CALM, ENJOY YOUR SELF ESTEEM.

MUCH RICHER THAN WHEN I STARTED, AS MY RECORDS WILL ACCOUNT,

TO CASH IN THE DULY NOTED, SHOULD ESTABLISH SAID AMOUNT.

WHAT'S GONE, IS NOW GONE, AND NOT RECOGNIZED AS FAULT,

LET'S NOW PURSUE THE OTHER SECRETS, LOCKED UP IN LIFE'S VAULT.

REMEMBERING AT "50", PUTTING MY PROTECTED THOUGHTS TO SONG,

"HALF MY LIFE HAS PASSED ME BY NOW", EXPRESSION HAS MADE ME STRONG.

LIVING THESE LAST "25 "YEARS, SOME MOMENTS DON'T COMPREHEND,

LIFE TRAVELS BY, IN THE WINK OF THE EYE, EMBRACE CHANGES, BEGIN AGAIN.

SIXTY EQUALS
(3 AND 9 AND 99)

I'M ALL IN FOR BASEBALL, THERE ARE MILLIONS WHO SHARE THE THOUGHT,

HUNDREDS WERE SPENT ON BALLS AND BATS, THE BASEBALL CARDS I BOUGHT.

THE PRESENCE OF THE HEROES, FOR ALL OF US TO SHARE,

ILLUMINATE OUR SPIRIT, THROUGH SOME DARK TIMES OF DESPAIR.

YOUR FAVORITE TEAM CONFOUNDS YOU, SHARING LOVE WHILE TOUCHING HATE,

ALL BECAUSE THE BALL IS ROUND, RESULTS COME DOWN TO FATE.

STATISTICS CHASE TO FIND CONTROL, OF WHAT A SCORE COULD BE,

A PERFECT SPHERE WITH LACES SEWN, AVERTS PREDICTABILITY.

RECORDS MADE ARE BROKEN, PLAYERS SUSTAIN THE PACE,

EVERY PITCH AND STRUCTURED MOVE, INTENSIFIES THE RACE.

OVERBEARING SUPERSTITIONS, PROVIDE SOME MAGIC FEEL,

ANYTHING TO UPHEAVE A JINX, FOR MOMENTS MADE MORE REAL.

WE FINISH WITH THE HOMER, A MOST THRILLING SIGHT TO SEE,

FUELS A GAME FOR "MILLIONS" SEATED, EVERY MOTION HISTORY.

SOME THOUGHTS ON DEATH

THE THING ABOUT DEATH,

ITS CONSCIENCE IS CLEAN.

OPERATING NON-STOP,

 A PRECISION MACHINE.

UNDAUNTED BY FEELINGS,

NO PRESSURE INVOLVED,

EVERY EPISODE COMPLETED,

NO SITUATION UNSOLVED.

FINAL CLOSURES TAKE TIME,

WE'RE ALL ON OUR OWN,

SOME PERSONS ONCE PRESENT,

WILL HOPEFULLY BE KNOWN.

THE CYCLE OF LIFE,

IS VICIOUS AT TIMES,

NEVER PAUSING AT EXCUSE,

JUST EXCELLS AT THE CLIMB.

WHEN CROSSING ITS PATH,

ALL OPTION WEIGHS LOW,

WHAT MIGHT HAVE BEEN,

YOU NEVER WILL KNOW.

TAKING DOWN THE CHRISTMAS TREE

TAKING DOWN THE CHRISTMAS TREE CAN BE QUITE A CHORE.

STANDING THERE, FOR ALL TO SEE, DECORATED AT THE DOOR.

BRIGHTLY LIT, UNTIL THE END, WE HATE TO SEE IT GO.

OUR SYMBOL OF THE SEASON TREND, IT SETS THE MOOD AGLOW.

I TAKE THE CLIPPERS TO THE LIMBS UNTIL THEY DISAPPEAR,

CUTTING EACH, AND EVERY BRANCH, WITH THOUGHTFUL CARE AND TEAR.

BRING THE PIECES TO THE CANAL, THEY SOON KEEP NEW LILLIES WARM,

TAKING ON A NEW ROLE, TO KEEP SPRING PLANTS FROM HARM.

THE DECORATIONS ARE PUT AWAY, TIL THE TIME WILL COME ONCE MORE,

TO STAND THE TREE SO STATELY, DECORATED AT THE DOOR.

THE BAKER'S DAUGHTER

SWEET NORMA JEAN, FRAGILE PRESENCE SO CLEAN,

TO BE LOVED, WAS MUCH, OF WHAT YOU WISHED FOR.

KEEPING INSIDE, ALL THOSE THOUGHTS YOU DENIED,

CARE FOR OTHERS, FORCING SOME DETOUR.

NOT SLEEPING, AWAKE, NIGHT AFTER NIGHT,

HOLDING THE WORLD ON YOUR SHOULDER,

WATCHING THE WORLD, QUICKLY IN FLIGHT,

NOT GETTING REAL LOVE, BUT JUST OLDER.

WHEN FINALLY, TO SLEEP, ALL ALONE YOU WILL KEEP,

YOUR THOUGHTS, AND ALL YOU INVISION.

FOREVER HOPING THAT SOMEONE WILL CALL OUT YOUR NAME,

TO ACCEPT THIS STUNNING LOSS, FROM POOR DECISION.

THEY WERE TOO LATE, IT'S FOR CERTAIN THEY FAILED,

SEEMS HOLLYWOOD LOST, THE BREADCRUMBS TO FOLLOW,

SO, WE'LL MEET YOUR DEMAND, FOR UNDERSTANDING AND LOVE,

WE SHOULD HAVE BEEN THERE, MAYBE LATE, BUT WE'RE HERE NOW.

NOW WE LOOK AT YOUR FACE, WE TOUCH PAPER SKIN,

WE THINK WE FEEL PAIN, AND WE HEAR YOU,

BITTERSWEET IS THE TASTE, AT TIMES WE'RE BEWILDERED,

IT'S NOT MUCH, BUT IT'S OUR WAY TO BE NEAR YOU.

THE GARAGE

AT EVERY CROSSROADS IN AMERICA, ALL SMALL TOWNS
HAVE A PLACE,

WHERE RULES AND INFORMATION, CHUGGING HUSBANDS
CAN BE TRACED.

THE KIDS BLOW UP THEIR TIRES, GET FREE SODAS FROM THE
"CREW",

WHERE CUSTOMERS AND THE TRAVELER, GAS UP, STRETCH
OUT, AND RENEW.

MANY ASK DIRECTIONS, OFTEN TIMES TO SHOP,

PEANUT MACHINES AND FIREBALLS, THEIR KIDS INSIST
THEY STOP.

BAY DOORS HANG WIDE OPEN, CARS UP ON THE LIFT,

THEIRS ALWAYS BEERS ON FRIDAY NIGHT AND THE LOCALS
ARE ALWAYS SWIFT.

THEY FORM COMMUNITY CENSUS, OUTREACH, AND
CONTROL,

ASSURE THE OUTLOOK FOR THE FUTURE, MAINTAIN TO
KEEP IT WHOLE.

EVERY VILLAGE HAS THEM, THOSE KEEPERS OF GOOD
FAITH,

IT'S MORE THAN THE "GARAGE", MORE THE " KEEPER OF
THE GATE".

THE RULE OF LAW

PRINCIPLES ARE RULES, TO SIMPLIFY COMPLICATIONS,

OVERRIDING GENERAL THOUGHT, FROM HARNASSED EDUCATION.

LEVELING LIFE'S PLAYING FIELD, WHEN OBJECTIVITY FAILS.

MEDIATING DISARRAY, WHEN ABSTRACT CHOICE PREVAILS.

INFORMATION WE COLLECTED, WITH OUR SEARCHES DOWN THE ROAD,

COMBINING THINGS THAT WORK, WITH WOUNDS OF THE UNKNOWN.

TRIALS, FEELINGS TESTED, CONFUSED IN THEIR ROUTINES,

THEIR CONTRIBUTIONS ARE WASTED, IN THE EFFORT OF THE MEANS.

BEGIN WITH SMALL CORRECTIONS, LIKE THE OCEANS ON THEIR SAND,

CHANGES GO UNNOTICED, AS THEY PURIFY THE PLAN.

OUR SAME OLD WAY OF DOING THINGS WILL TEST US ON ITS OWN,

PRESENT US, AS WE STRUGGLE ON, WITH WHAT HAS NOT YET SHOWN.

TEMPORARY, TO KEEP THINGS WORKING, IS HEALTHY TO A LIMIT,

POLITICAL EFFORTS, MADE IN HASTE, EXPECT LOSS OF WORTH WITHIN IT.

LAWS ARE THE RESULTS OF PRINCIPLES, SUPPORTING STRUGGLE FOR ITS FATE,

FOREVER WILL THE PROCESS LIVE, PRESENTING CHANGES FOR DEBATE.

TIMELINES

FOREVER IT'S BEEN WITH THOSE TIMELINES,

THOSE FRIENDS, LOVERS, THAT PLEASURE, AND PAIN.

PUSHING THOSE LIMITS CAUSES CONFLICT,

TIL THE DOMINANT CHARACTERS REMAIN.

THE LINES, THEY BECOME SO MUCH THINNER,

THE MORE THAT YOU UTILIZE TIME,

WHEN THE FRUSTRATION, DECLARES THERE'S A WINNER,

ARE YOU HAPPY WITH THAT SIDE OF THE LINE?

SO CLOSE IS THE PAIN, AND PLEASURE OF LIFE,

AND INDEED SO, WITH OUR LOVE, AND OUR HATE.

AS LONG AS THERE'S TIME, TO WITHDRAW FROM OUR
CHOICE,

THE FINAL CHOICE FOR DECISION LEAVES FATE.

WHEN DOWN TO THE WIRE, SATISFACTION CAN BE SHADE,

THE CHOICE WE ACCEPT MAY BE GREY,

THE CHANCES WE TAKE, WITH OUR DECISIONS WITH TIME,

FORCE US TO BLEND, AS THE TIMELINES CONVEY.

THE TOWERS HAVE FALLEN (9-11-01)

WE WAITED ALL DAY FOR THEIR CALLS,

IT SEEMED YEARS WENT BY WITHOUT WORDS.

UNTIL THIS MOMENT WE NEVER KNEW,

HOW PRECIOUS THEIR VOICE IS TO BE HEARD.

DON'T GO, YOU CAN'T LEAVE NOW,

THERE IS SO MUCH MORE WE NEED TO SAY,

PLEASE, GOD, DON'T LET THEM LEAVE NOW,

WE CAN'T BEAR THAT THEY'VE GONE AWAY.

WHY DO WE FIGHT, AND HURT ONE ANOTHER,

TAKE THE LIVES, OF OUR SISTERS AND BROTHERS,

WHO DECIDES, WHO LIVES AND DIES IN THIS WORLD,

AND WHAT POWER DECIDES WHO IS RIGHT?

IT WILL NEVER BE OVER, TO THE POINT THAT WE'RE EVEN,

WHAT DECLARES WHO THE WINNER WILL BE?

NOT THE SCALES OF JUSTICE, OR A WEALTH OF NATIONS,

LET US HOPE FOR A UNIVERSE OF DIVINITY.

THE WEDDING OF MOTHER NATURE

SUMMER, WINTER, FALL, AND SPRING,

PRESENT MOTHER NATURES WEDDING RING.

THEY HONOR ALL HER WONDEROUS WAYS,

GUIDE HER THROUGH ALL MORTAL GAZE.

ASSAULTED BY ALL SIDES WITH PAIN,

WHAT IS IT MORTALS HOPE TO GAIN?

REVITALIZING WITH INTENT SO PURE,

THE WRONGS DONE TO HER, BECOME OBSCURE.

RECOGNIZED ARE WRONGS UPON OCCASION,

UNTRUTHS, MISDEEDS, AND DISTURBING ABRASION.

ON WHAT HAS BEEN REIGNED, FOR ALL TO REAP,

OFTEN ROBBED WHEN WE'RE ASLEEP.

KNOWLEDGE SIFTED FOR ADVANTAGE AND HARM,

INVENT WORDS OF HALF TRUTHS, INITIATE ALARM.

REBELLING ATTACKS, ON HER RESOURCE AND RIGHTS,

TRUTH FORWARD MARCHES, WITH CONVICTION AND FIGHT.

THE MARRIAGE TO CHANGES WILL BALANCE IT ALL,

HER POSTURE IS IMMORTAL, NEVER NEED FOR RECALL.

THE WORDS ARE NOW EXPLAINED

A LIFETIME OF THESE FEELINGS, SO DEEP AND UNRECOGNIZED,

ALL THESE TIMES SURPRESSING JOYS, AWKWARD AGONIZED.

EXPRESSION SEEKING CONDUIT, LEFT TUMBLING, CAST ASIDE,

MY POETRY, PROSE, AND FLOWING LYRICS, I FORCED THEM TO SUBSIDE.

NOT KNOWING THAT A GIFT FOR WORDS COULD NURTURE SOMEONE'S SOUL,

GATHERED PIECES FOR PARTS UNKNOWN ARE GLUED TO MAKE THEM WHOLE.

OFTEN SQUASHING IMPULSE, NOT LIGHTING CREATIVE SPARK,

WASTING CREATIVITY, NEVER TO EMBARK.

REBELLION, NAI'VETE', IGNORANCE, AND YOUTH,

WOULD PASS AND TAKE ITS TOLL, REVEAL AT LAST THE TRUTH.

EMOTIONS, FEELINGS, ACTIONS, AND FACTS, PASS THROUGH VERSE AND RHYME,

RECOGNIZED BY MANY, WRITTEN RECORD FOR ALL TIME.

THOUGHTS IN THE DEVELOPMENT STAGES

PAINSTAKING REJECTION FUELS GREATNESS

FAILURE IS THE PEA UNDER THE MATTRESS OF SUCCESS.

TRUTH IS OBSCURRED FROM NEED, AND CONVENIENTLY NAVIGATED BY NECESSITY.

HAVOC IS "BLACK NOISE"

PEACE OF MIND ARRIVES IN MODERATION, ON PILLARS OF HONOR, EMPATHY, HUMILITY, AND RESPECT.

PEACE OF MIND IS A NEVER-ENDING SEARCH FOR WHAT YOU THINK IT TO BE

THE WORLD SHARES A "LITTLE BLACK BOOK"

WATER OVER THE DAM OFTEN TRICKLES SOMEWHERE TO MAKE A RETURN TRIP

SECRETS WILL HIDE IN A BLACK HOLE FOR ETERNITY UNTIL DISCOVERY

TURNING THE CORNER

TURNING THE CORNER, MOVING WITH A SMILE,

TURNING THE CORNER, IN A LIFE THAT'S WELL WORTHWHILE.

I'M TRAVELING ON THE BACKSIDE, COUNTING EVERY DAY,

I'VE BEEN WORKING FOR QUITE A WHILE, ON THIS LIFE HIGHWAY.

GLIDING THROUGH SOME HISTORY, TO SOME MAIN EVENTS,

I CAN STILL RECALL TO YOU, PRECIOUS MOMENTS SPENT.

NOW I CAN SEE A CHANGE IN ROUTE, SEE SOME DIRECTIONS UP AHEAD,

MY CHANCE TO MAKE SOME MEMORIES, WHILE GOING AROUND THE BEND.

TURNING THE CORNER, THE FIRST TURN THAT I SEE,

INTO THE FIRST STRAIGHT AWAY, HAPPY AS CAN BE.

SECOND CORNER, CAME AND WENT, LIKE SOME SOUTHBOUND TRAIN,

I'M NOW INTO MY FINAL TURN AND KEEP ON GOING ONCE AGAIN.

TURNING THE CORNER GOING ROUND THE BEND,

TURNING AROUND THE CORNER, WON'T LET IT EVER END.

KEEPING ON THE THROTTLE, POURING ON THE SPEED,

TURNING THE CORNER, I HAVE BEEN ALL IN ON WHERE IT LEADS.

EVERYBODY'S HAD THAT DREAM,

LIVIN LIFE FULL, ALL THE WHILE,

YOU HEAD INTO LIFE CORNERS,

 HOPE TO COME OUT WITH A SMILE.

PARADISE IS A FOUR LANE HIGHWAY

THE BASHAKILL

QUIET FLOWING, DARKENED WATER, GLACIER FORMED,
SUSTAINED BY STORM AND MOUNTAIN SPRINGS,
NURTURING LIFE FORMS, PLANTS AND FISH, AS BIRDS
CREATE WHITE NOISE AND WHISPERING BACKROUNDS.

THE TOWPATH

ACROSS THE WATER NEARBY FOLLOWING CLOSELY ON THE
FAR HIGH BANK, A WIDE PATH THROUGH THE LANDSCAPE,
MATCHING EVERY NATURAL CURVE ABOVE THE BASIN OF
AQUATIC BEAUTY, STRUCTURED AS A PART OF A MUCH
LARGER PLAN, ENCOURAGING HARMONY WITH ALL ITS
BREATHLESS SURROUNDINGS.

THE O&W RAIL TRAIL

REMNANTS OF THE RAILS AND TIES SO STURDY, LONG
ENDURING THE ONETIME PASSENGER AND FREIGHT,
ENAMORED IN IMPORTANCE, NOW REPLACED WITH A
HIGHER STANDARD OF GRACE AND SANCTUARY,
ENDLESSLY WANDERS THROUGH SPECTACULAR DISPLAYS
OF PICTURESQUE NATURAL WONDER, COMPLIMENTING ITS
FUTURE IMPORTANCE.

INDIAN ORCHARD ROAD

COMES THE LAST VENTURE, NOT LEAST TO ITS TRAVELER,
WINDING ABOVE ALL OTHER GLORIOUS OPTIONS TO THE
SAME DESTINATIONS, LESS RESISTANT TO OTHER CHOICES,
STILL IT PROVIDES MAJESTIC OPTICS OF BEAUTY AND
CHALLENGES THAT BLEND TO COMBINE ALL DECISIONS

MADE TO BE JOYOUS FOR ADMIRATION TO NATURE. HARDENED BY TREADED MOVEMENT AND CONSTANT REPETITIVE WEIGHTED OBJECTS REFLECTING THE ELEMENTS OF ALL SEASONS TO PROVIDE ANOTHER WAY HOME.

LIFE AS I SEE IT

LIFE IS ALWAYS IN ATTACK, NEVER SEDENDARY,

A PERPETUATING MACHINE, AVOIDING THE ORDINARY.

CONDUCTING SOME CONTEST TO ALTER THE BALANCE,

PROVIDING ALL ADJUSTMENTS FOR THE MIXTURE OF THE CHALLENGE.

NEVER TIRED, NOR DONE, EVER SUBJECT TO SLEEP,

AN UNENDING FORCE, ON THE CLIMB BEYOND STEEP.

EXPOSING THE CHOICES TOWARDS A WORLD OF DELIGHT,

WHILE PRESENTING ITS AVENUES OF HORROR AND FRIGHT.

LEADING FORWARDS AND BACKWARDS TOGETHER IN STEP,

AT THE SAME TIME IT STOPS YOU, CONFUSED WITH CONCEPT.

IT LIMITS THE COMMON SENSE, WHILE ENTICING IN CHARM,

WHILE RAGING IN ARGUMENT, OVERFLOWING WITH HARM.

YOUR HEAD CAN BE BLEEDING INSIDE WITH YOUR THOUGHTS,

BAD DECISIONS ARE COSTLY, IF THEY ARE NOT CAUGHT.

BACK AND FORTH IS THE PENDULUM, UP AND DOWN IS THE FORCE,

OVER THE BATTLEFIELDS OF HURT, YOU'LL BE SUBJECT TO ENDORCE.

YOU ENCOUNTER SOME STRAIGHTAWAYS, THEN TWIST INTO TURN,

RECOGNIZING IN THE JOURNEY, WE ARE WHAT WE EARN.

COLLECTING YOUR EXPERIENCE FOR A LIBRARY OF TRIAL,

WILL COMFORT THOSE GOLDEN YEARS, AND REDUCE SOME DENIAL.

THE REMINDER THAT A SECOND CHANCE MAY LINGER TO TAKE,

OVERALL, WITH THE ODDS AT HAND, WILL REPAIR A MISTAKE.

PRESENTED AND NEVER EQUAL, LIFE BEGINS AND YOU EXIST,

HOPEFUL EACH AND EVERYONE RESPONDS TO THE ASSIST.

UNNERVING AND PEACEFUL, MISDIRECTED TO THE END,

A PLAYBOOK, A RESOURCE, UNHARNESSED AS FRIEND.

www.ingramcontent.com/pod-product-compliance
Lightning Source LLC
Chambersburg PA
CBHW051527120626
46551CB00012B/1108